HEAL TO LEAD

Raven + Grace

Contents

A Gift from the Authors

Throughout this book, we've shared powerful tools and practices that have guided us on our healing journeys, empowering us to lead with strength and purpose. Now, we want to extend these resources to you.

We've created a collaborative digital workbook filled with valuable tools to support your own journey to accompany this book. Inside this digital workbook, you'll find journal prompts to help you gain clarity, guided meditations to nurture your soul, and transformational educational videos designed to inspire your growth. To download, visit https://ravenandgrace.com/healtolead1.

It's our hope that these resources will enrich your experience and support you on your path to healing and leadership.

With heartfelt gratitude,
The Authors of Heal to Lead

HEAL TO LEAD

Introduction

JENNIFER GRACE

If you're a leader or on the brink of stepping into your full potential as one, this book was crafted for you.

As a transformational trainer with more than seventeen years of experience working alongside leaders, I have learned one undeniable truth: You cannot effectively lead until you have properly healed.

Time and again, I've witnessed passionate individuals who feel called to serve and lead stumble. They yearn to share their message and voice, but imposter syndrome, self-doubt, and a lack of self-worth often silence them.

They freeze.

Or they muster the courage to step forward—hands sweating, knees shaking, hearts pounding—only to retreat at the first sign of rejection. Their inner critic, loud and unyielding, shouts, "Who do you think you are? You're not cut out for this. Go home and play it safe."

Sadly, they listen.

When this happens, I ask, "Could there be any unresolved trauma that you haven't dealt with yet?"

The answer is almost always yes.

The good news is there are countless ways to heal.

In this book, twenty-four leaders use their courage and authenticity to share their journeys of healing and the techniques and practices that helped them lead from a place of wholeness. We are a collective of coaches, healers, and experts, and now, published authors, who have done the work to step up—hands sweating, knees shaking, hearts beating—and share our stories of moving from darkness to light. Our hope is that you will feel inspired to do the same.

We are dedicated to making a difference in your life. Like a pebble creating ripples in a pond, we aim to illuminate your path, so one day, you too can shine your light and create ripples that touch others.

This book is the first in a trilogy, with one-hundred percent of the net proceeds dedicated to breaking the cycles of trauma and healing the world. For *Heal to Lead: Stories To Turn Your Wounds Into Wisdom* Volume One, we chose the Nashville Center for Sexual Assault as our beneficiary.

Thank you in advance for helping us be the change we all want to see.

One

Two Wheels and a Mountain of Faith

The Muse Within: Pursuing
Self-Inspiration

SHAUNA KELLY

W *hat are you doing with your life? What are you **really** doing with your life?!*
Where is the adventure?

I'm panic stricken in the middle of the night. I'm overcome with a feeling that if I died tomorrow, the regrets I would have would be immense, as echoed by the questions I keep asking myself over and over in my head. The stories people would share about me at my funeral would be dull and run-of-the-mill.

Not like the stories relayed through tears and sad laughter only hours before at my father's wake. Tales of wild and sometimes strange adventures on hiking, skiing, and fishing adventures, hi-jinks in the recreational sports leagues he haunted for decades, inspirational leadership throughout his dedicated career, and his ability to tell a great story to gales of laughter.

I always felt there was a quietness about my dad, a calming force hidden behind practical jokes and an inquisitive mind. It was a contrast to the sometimes volatile emotional environment of the rest of my family; my mom and my older twin sisters were often in some kind of conflict with loud red-headed energy. I think this overshadowed the perception I had of my father and what was really happening in his life.

This misconception came through loud and clear at his funeral, which was attended by so many people it was standing room only. It was a large venue and it was packed. I was amazed at the number of mourners who had come from every area of his life, both professionally and part of his personal pursuits. Person after person came up to me to recount what an amazing man he had been and what an impact he made on them, either directly or through observing the adventures he had in his life. My dad loved to take on new things and never thought age was a barrier. This showed up in activities like back-country skiing once a year with a group half his age, or taking up snowboarding at the age of sixty (something we did together when I was twenty-five).

As the funeral led into the wake, I was seeing my dad for who he truly was: quiet by nature, but living loudly. All in. I was in awe of all he had done but even more so by how he moved so many people.

This epiphany about my father is what led to the heart-racing panic attack I was having in bed at three in the morning. Here was my dad who had travelled the world, excelled in his career, and spent every other waking moment experiencing adventure in the great outdoors, and what was I doing? Would my kids ever be inspired by my life?

In addition to the flooding grief over the loss of my father, a growing sadness washed over me that I was going nowhere. Not only was my life not going to inspire those around me, more importantly it was not even close to inspiring myself.

I have always considered adventure to be one of my core values. Not necessarily 'jumping out of a plane' kind of adventure, but 'hiking up tall mountains and looking out over lakes and valleys' kind of adventure. Doing big things outside in nature that get your heart pumping and the blood flowing. Pushing myself to places that make me feel alive in the moment. Where I feel like I'm standing on top of the world.

My dad was definitely a mountain man. Nature was his church, which is why I grew up camping, hiking, fishing, and skiing. Every weekend, we would load into the old brown station wagon and head to the nearby Rocky Mountains. Like my dad, I realized at an early age I could find great moments of accomplishment alongside solace in natural spaces. Standing on a high mountain ridge looking down upon a glacier-fed lake—those blue-green waters sparkling back up at me with such beauty and calmness—always brings on the feeling that I'm part of something greater and so alive.

I was thirty-seven when my dad passed away and into a three-year marriage to my best friend and husband. We had a one-year-old and our growing family was one of joy and comfort. But reflecting on all that I had done in my twenties and early thirties, it seemed like there were more hangovers and less adventures. My progressive trajectory was repeatedly heading for the couch, accompanied by a dwindling enthusiasm for my working life, and a growing sense of overwhelm with everything else. Adventure was fading into the background.

For the sake of my happiness and my mental well-being, I needed to get back outside. I needed to save myself from oblivion by getting back to the mountains.

TWO WHEELS AND A MOUNTAIN OF FAITH

I forgot to mention my love for biking. When I was kid, I found freedom pedalling throughout our neighborhood and around the pathways near our house. I could escape the sometimes chaotic noise of my house and head to wherever, just riding my troubles away. My body was naturally comfortable on a bike. I was one with two wheels.

One of the first things I found attractive about my husband was his love for mountain biking and skiing. He fit the bill of someone who liked to get outside, and I knew that was something I needed in any long-term relationship to which I was going to say, "I do."

Although mountain biking was something I hadn't really ever done before, it was something I was intrigued by and always wanted to try. So, this was where I focused my attention when I wanted to build some adventure back into my life. I asked my mom for my dad's mountain bike and got my husband, Chris, to start taking me out on the trails. It wasn't long before I signed up for a women's weekend mountain bike camp to improve my skills and confidence. I was sure I would be intimidated by all the other experienced riders, but I found a welcoming community who was excited to share the stoke of their sport and have a new member to join them.

My newfound passion turned out to be the perfect combination of riding a bicycle and exploring in the mountains. Riding through forested trails, pushing my physical limitations by riding up and over roots and rocks, then the reward of the fast and flowy downhills, all of it was lighting me up and making me grin from ear to ear.

I joined a women's mountain biking club and made a whole new community of friends who shared the same enthusiasm and appreciation for the outdoors. On a whim in 2014, my husband and I completed a four-day mountain bike stage race. We loved it so much we have participated in one every year since, travelling all over North America to challenge ourselves and reconnect with the biking community.

Mountain biking literally saved me from the dark hole I was falling into, the place I could feel myself being absorbed by that early morning I took stock of my life after my father's wake. It was the missing piece of the puzzle of me—the one that brought together my love for biking and the great outdoors. It has challenged me and rewarded me. Most importantly, it has guided me to a place of self-love and appreciation.

PURSUING SELF-INSPIRATION

You know those itches you get on occasion? The ones where you are drawn to something for what seems like an unknown reason? It's founded on an attraction we have no explanation for—it just keeps coming back to our attention over and over again.

Sometimes we venture to try whatever thing distracts us, and sometimes we find something that becomes truly influential in our lives. Or, maybe it doesn't take hold as a hobby or a repeated interest. In those cases, it's the avenue that leads us to the next shiny interest and then something after that. Eventually, through an intricate web of random interests, we find ourselves knee deep in a love we can't let go of—a genuine passion project. Something that ignites a fire.

This was mountain biking for me. If you had told me earlier in my life that it would be one of my obsessions in my forties and fifties, I would have laughed. It seemed like such an extreme sport to me and I didn't identify as that speed of person.

But I was always intrigued by it. There was a curiosity about the sport and it kept crossing my path in indirect ways. I'm glad I finally paid attention because it is a significant component of my identity at fifty-five: I am a mother, wife, friend, daughter, sister, writer, transformational coach, and a mountain biker.

Finding mountain biking became the perfect recipe for reconnecting with my love of the freedom of two wheels and the hug and comfort of the mountain spirit. Making the effort to become more skilled at mastering all my bike could do and getting out to practice on the trails was next to no effort because it blended two long-term foundational loves of mine: biking and the outdoors.

These are the paths you need to start walking in your life. What interests you? Better yet, what is trying to get your attention? Try it. Explore it. If it fades away, watch where it leads you next. What draws your eye?

Don't be baffled by the calling if it seems confusing. Maybe it's an artistic endeavour like drawing or glass blowing, or an instrument that your fingers imagine they play. Maybe the music of a foreign language makes you feel slightly electric and you find yourself wanting to learn certain words or phrases. These practices are calling to you for a reason. You owe it to yourself to be curious why. These are the moments that offer opportunities for self-discovery and reflection.

Don't let the naysayers get in your way. There may be well-meaning friends and family who don't understand what you are up to—if you don't understand it, why would they? I heard all kinds of things like,"Mountain biking?! Isn't that a guy's sport where they break their bones running into trees?"

Trust your intuition and follow it. In hindsight, you will always see the reason why you were drawn to take on something new. I ride with many biking friends, male and female, and injuries are always considered a badge of honour in our community!

The other popular voice that will try to keep you from new interests is your friendly Negative Nelly that resides in your head. The one who says he/she doesn't want you to get hurt or look bad to others.

Are you out of your mind thinking about taking a watercolours class? You have no artistic talent! The guitar?! Remember that everyone knows you don't have any rhythm.

When I was in my twenties, I was friends with several mountain bikers. Even then, I felt an itch of intrigue about the sport, but all I heard in my head was *Shauna! You're not as fit as they are. You're not even that athletic, and they have way more stoke and energy than you do.*

I thought I was not skilled enough, weighed too much, was too slow, and on and on.

As I took up the sport in my late thirties, I learned to ignore those lies. Everyone is a beginner when they start something new. Skills come with practice. You will find your own speed, and being the fastest is not always what everything is about: It's about the enjoyment. Your body will rise to the occasion, and usually there is no required "look" or body type. There are no rules, and if there are, maybe you will be the first to break them.

These activities we can't get enough of will bring you joy and that's the most valuable experience you can have in life. These 'lights of your life' may not be your careers or even all consuming, but you know it is essential to your well-being to create time and space to explore these pursuits as they will bring out your inspirational gifts to yourself and others.

My passion for mountain biking has brought clarity to all of life's lessons, all the ups and downs. The trek up the trail may be a slog, but the reward of the surrounding beauty when you arrive at the top of the mountain and that sweaty sense of achievement makes every cell in my body shout, "This is living!"

Hard work brings reward. Crashes happen, and I have learned how to protect myself when I sense I'm about to hit the dirt. More importantly, I have conditioned myself to take a deep breath and find the calm, dust off my shorts, then get back on my bike and ride again.

If I had listened to the voices who said mountain biking was not for me, I would have missed one of the most pivotal opportunities I've experienced for personal growth. I would have missed fantastic friends who cheer me on with immense amounts of encouragement. I might still be looking for a reconnection to the mountains and laying on the couch. I am so grateful I followed my curiosity.

The Shauna I am today is not the panicked Shauna from almost twenty years ago. She tried something out of character and today feels more courageous and confident in herself.

She found the inspiration she was seeking. It was in herself all along.

Two

Beyond Blame

How Accepting Responsibility For Our Lives Changes Everything

HEATHER EVERETT

"Only when we are brave enough to explore the darkness will we discover the infinite power of our light."
Dr. Brené Brown

Before I understood the power of accountability, my life was a whirlwind of excuses and misplaced blame. I was convinced my struggles were someone else's fault—the boss who didn't appreciate me, the narcissistic mother who mistreated me, the romantic partners who didn't understand me, the family who let me down. It was a comfortable narrative that kept me safe from an uncomfortable truth: *I played a pivotal role in the outlook of my life experiences.* In other words, I was responsible for the life I was living.

This realization began to appear in May 2020, two months into the global Covid-19 pandemic. I had been feeling the effects of the one-two punch of breaking up with my boyfriend and being estranged from my mother. All I had were days and days filled with nothing but time to dwell on what I didn't have, and all of the ways I was wronged by others. One Monday morning, while standing in front of my bathroom mirror getting ready for yet another work Zoom call that felt devoid of purpose, I took a long look at the tired, sad, and lost person staring back at me. Reaching up to touch my cheeks, I was surprised by the damp skin under my fingertips.

Why am I crying?

The response from deep inside was quick and powerful.

Because you are choosing these experiences. You are choosing to be the victim in your story. You can choose to respond differently and be the hero in your story.

While I'd like to say that accepting this truth was easy and effortless, that would be a lie. Similar to someone dealing with addiction, sometimes things have to get worse before they get better. I fell into a deep depression, struggling to find the energy to get out of bed each day. On weekends when my children were with their dad, I didn't get out of bed at all. I went from blaming everyone else to blaming myself, self-judgment wrapping itself around every thought. It was emotional warfare and I was losing the battle. I felt like I was sitting at an intersection trying to decide which direction to go, paralyzed by the fear of making yet another wrong choice, while the horns of other vehicles trumpeted around me.

The turning point came one day when I woke up, stared at the ceiling, and said to myself, *What's the point? I am just going to screw everything up again.*

Once again, a voice from deep inside stated with clear confidence, *You're the point. Do something. Anything.*

Before I thought too much about it, I picked up the phone and texted my friend who had a home gym in her garage and asked if I could workout with her a few days a week.

She immediately replied with an enthusiastic, "Yes!"

At the time, I had no idea that this seemingly insignificant decision would serve as a catalyzing moment in my life.

The first few weeks in her garage were a blur of tears and sweat as she pushed my body to its physical limits, and I pushed myself to my emotional limits. Slowly, but surely, I started to let go of all the stories I believed about myself and others. I was working my emotional, mental, and physical muscles in a way I had never experienced before, and it started to transform everything I said, did, and felt.

I first started seeing how the strength and self-trust I gained in those workouts created powerful moments in my career. What had once been an area of my life where things happened **to** me, a place where I was more than happy to play the victim, slowly became an area where things happened **for** me. My relationships with colleagues evolved as they came to appreciate my willingness to take responsibility for my actions. They were inspired by my calm and steady way of being and began asking me what I did to shift my outlook. I was seen as a valuable leader in the company who was trusted to counsel my team, colleagues in other departments, and senior leadership on professional and personal challenges.

Most importantly, I began to see myself as the valuable leader of my life. The more I trusted the voice deep inside, what I refer to as my intuition or inner knowing, the more I trusted myself to know what to do next. The more I thought about what to do next, the more I felt called to help others become the heroes in their stories. I went back to school and became a certified master life coach and mindfulness workshop facilitator, applying the skills I learned both at work and at home. In July 2022, I made the decision to shift away from my near twenty-year career in marketing and move towards entrepreneurship in the world of wellness and personal growth.

At the same time, accountability started to reshape my personal life. One key aspect of accountability is setting boundaries based on your personal values, or as author and famed shame researcher, Dr. Brené Brown refers to them as "your what's okay/what's not okay". I chose the word **reshape** when describing what happens when we set boundaries because when we take stock of who and what is in our lives, and decide what stays and what goes, our worlds morph into something different.

NAVIGATING BOUNDARIES

While a lot of what happened during my initial boundary setting was positive, I also experienced a lot of loss because my values no longer aligned with the values of others in my life. When I chose to stop drinking after years of establishing myself as a fun party girl and wine industry professional, my social life shifted overnight. Friends and family didn't know how to interact with me without alcohol. It was disconcerting, but it did not weaken my resolve. I knew that in order to have full ownership of my life, I needed the clarity of sobriety. I also knew that the relationships that were meant to exist in my life would manifest as long as I continued to manifest the life I wanted to experience.

The thing about living an accountable life is you start paying more attention to your actions and inactions, and the consequences of your decisions on yourself and others. You start seeing the world around you as connective tissue that you can choose to strengthen or atrophy. You start to notice the little intricacies of life you once missed, and you begin to realize the world around you has been waiting for you to sit up and take notice, waiting for you to recognize your unique gifts. You realize that you, exactly as you are, flaws and all, are exactly what the world needs. The world doesn't need us to try to be more like each other, but rather it needs us to celebrate and appreciate our differences. No matter where we were born or what we have, we are all still precious souls that entered this world as small, defenseless, curious, and hopeful babies.

This powerful truth helped me step toward my mother after being estranged for almost three years. In short, my relationship with my mother was complicated. My choice to separate from her was a necessary but difficult decision, especially in the midst of her serious health crisis. I just didn't know how to have a relationship with her and with myself at the same time. I had to put on my own oxygen mask first. Looking back, I know this decision was the first step toward taking responsibility for my own life, as well as the first step toward reuniting us.

The call from my ex-husband came in the middle of a stormy January night. When I walked away from the relationship, he had stepped up to help her navigate the disarray of the senior health care system, becoming her unofficial medical proxy. As he told me the details of her situation in the hospital with complications from type 2 diabetes and doctors thinking she wouldn't make it through the night, my mind was quiet and my body still. After we hung up, I stared at the ceiling and asked myself, *What do I want to do?*

A minute or two passed and no answer came. I stayed in silent meditation, heart racing, knowing it would. Suddenly, without realizing what I was doing, I started to get dressed. I was going to see her.

The two-hour drive to the hospital was slow, rain coming down in buckets, roads flooded, shoulders littered with cars that had spun out of control. It felt apocalyptic, which felt apropos for the journey. Mother Nature displayed the torrent of emotions flowing through my body.

What would it be like to see her? What would I say? What would it be like to sit next to her? Would she know I was there?

A phone call with the nurses station answered some of my questions. My mother had Covid and was in quarantine. I could sit outside her room, but there would be no physical contact. Sometimes we place the boundaries; other times the boundaries are placed for us. When

I arrived, it was clear that her body was in distress. Nurses moving quickly around her bed, adjusting IVs, monitors beeping, my mother's eyes unfocused and full of uncertainty. I sat outside her room and silently repeated to myself, *I forgive you. I forgive me. I wish you peace.*

Several hours later, her condition improved and I knew she would live to see another day. I also knew I would visit her again. The estrangement was over. She was different and so was I. It was time to create the space to help heal our hearts.

I saw her a few more times over the following months. She met my boyfriend, we called her sister, I fed her, and we watched her favorite game shows. As her condition continued to deteriorate, there were less and less words, and more and more comfortable silences. When hospice called to say she wasn't doing well and believed she would transition soon, my son and I jumped in the car and made our way to her. Everything was different about this trip. The June weather was clear and beautiful, traffic was light, and my heart was unburdened by the fears and doubts of the past.

My last moments with her were spent telling her how much I loved her and how I knew she did the best she could with the tools she had available to her. Once again, I silently repeated the mantra from the hospital, *I forgive you. I forgive me. I wish you peace.* This time feeling the shift in both of us, feeling the letting go.

Early the next day while walking in the cool morning air, I got the call. She had transitioned. As I crumpled to the ground, the grief overwhelming my body, I felt such gratitude for the emotions I was feeling and for the work I had done. It had prepared me for that moment and all the moments before it. I was able to embrace responsibility for my half of our story, unlock my heart to true forgiveness, and share genuine love.

THE MAGIC OF ACCOUNTABILITY

Living life with accountability has transformed me in ways I can't fully express in writing. I am more confident, more self-aware, and more at peace with myself. I have learned that taking responsibility for my actions doesn't mean placing blame on myself for everything that goes wrong; it means recognizing the role I play and taking steps to make it better. It means letting go of the need to control everything and everyone around me.

The emotional impact on my life has been profound. I no longer feel like a victim of my circumstances. Instead, I feel empowered to shape my own destiny. I have learned to forgive myself for my past mistakes and view them as opportunities for growth. My relationships are healthier, my work is more fulfilling, and my sense of self-worth is stronger than ever.

Accountability is about leading our life and our happiness. It's about discovering that the power to change our circumstances already exists inside of us. It is an exploration into our darkness that requires vulnerability, courage, and love. It is a journey toward our immeasurable light.

Journaling became an important facet of my awareness practice. I invite you to invest in a beautiful journal and pen, and take the time to reflect on your own life. Consider where you might be avoiding accountability. What excuses are you making? Where are you placing blame on others? Practice letting go of self-judgment and embrace your curiosity.

Ask yourself, *What is one small step I can take toward becoming the hero in my story?* Then stay still and listen for the answer that already exists inside of you.

Three

Calling You In...Not Out!

The Shift from External Blame to Internal Responsibility

KIM HERRLEIN

It began as a whisper...*Call Grandma, protect mommy.*

My earliest memories are tainted with fear. At five years old, I was in the darkness of my parents' downstairs bedroom, shaking as I dialed the phone. Upstairs my father, intoxicated and menacing, argued with my emotionally unhinged mother. Their cursing and screaming, punctuated by flying tchotchkes, crescendoed into chaos. In a flash, his thundering footsteps pounded as he descended to find me with the phone in my hand as I tried to get help.

His fury exploded. "Are you calling the cops?" a loaded threat hung in the air.

My tiny, scared, desperate voice trembled as I replied, "No, I'm calling Grandma."

"Put the phone down, or you'll see your blood all over these walls."

Chilled by his threat, I was left with an eternal scar because I knew the danger was real. Known for the pistol strapped to his ankle, he seemed to take demented pleasure in cleaning and brandishing his weapons while inebriated. Though many details have faded, I remember in detail deciding to stay away from him and their fights. Years later, I realized that his behavior may have been driven by a desperate grasp for any sense of power he felt he had.

From that day forward, I feared his wrath and found myself hiding in a locked bathroom, too many times to count, whilst their subconscious demons danced, again and again. I begged God to go home, even though I was already there.

With my acute sensitivity to the emotional needs of those around me, I became aware of the vulnerabilities within my family and understood that family was shrouded in secrecy. With hesitation, I accepted my role and took on the responsibility of being a source of comfort and solace for my mother. This accountability was not a burden but rather a natural extension of my awareness and acceptance of my family's needs. It was a childlike form of responsibility, filled with the innocence of offering a hug or a smile, people pleasing with good grades and accomplishments as I grew, yet it carried the weight of understanding that my presence mattered. I appreciated that. I learned to value the power of emotional support and the importance of being present for those we love. I loved my mom, my brother, and my grandparents.

THE WHISPER BECOMES A MURMUR...MOVE AWAY, PROTECT YOURSELF.

My college years couldn't have come soon enough, and despite my mother's plea to apply to New York local colleges, I rebelled. I went behind her back, applied, and was accepted to Boston University. At seventeen years old, I left the day-to-day routines and toxic cycles of my homelife. I gained awareness about just how dysfunctional my family truly was; however, I'm not out yet, as the darkness follows me. During college, I struggled with discipline and balancing the academic responsibility and newfound freedom. The 'party' atmosphere led me down a frightening path, one of substance abuse and promiscuity. For the first time in my academic life, I spiral and flunk out of school. I hid this from my parents, appealed to the department, and was given another chance. I accepted responsibility and embarked on a journey to learn more about family dynamics to comprehend my childhood's emotional impact.

I pursued psychology and communications with a revitalized vigor. Eager to learn about the subconscious, co-dependent relationships, inner child work, enmeshment styles, archetypes, alcoholism, passive-aggressive communication, domestic abuse, all of it. I grasped the concepts and applied the teachings.

It was the first time I took responsibility for my life and it was a game-changer. It's easy to blame external circumstances or other people for our problems, but doing so leaves us powerless. Accountability means recognizing that we always have a choice in how we respond to life's challenges. It means owning our actions and their consequences.

I appreciated my passion for learning and desire to shift my perspective from victim to victor. I recognized my role, understood the mission, and graduated with a desire to break familial patterns, to help serve and heal others. I knew this information could help my mom take control of her life and heal our deep-seated issues. With newfound courage, I chose to end an unhealthy relationship with my best friend. I was also accepted into graduate school in New York, ready to start anew even though I was headed back home.

THE MURMUR EXCLAIMS...RETURN HOME AND PROTECT YOURSELF.

I spent many late nights with mommy engaged in lively conversations, identifying our origin of trust issues, sharing techniques to modify our behaviors, aware that we lacked clear boundaries, and learned how to accept others while drawing boundaries. We primarily focused on choosing healthy assertive communication to express our needs. We teared up, we sobbed, and even laughed uncomfortably at the stark truths. I analyzed my behavior, as well as those closest to us, and demonstrated how I severed my ties, choosing love for myself over another. It was so promising, a time filled with hope. She was riveted. I was ecstatic. I thought I held the key to her happiness and fulfillment. My father resented it.

It was too late.

Years trapped in a lifeless marriage, overworked, and under appreciated, her body kept the score, and within five months of my homecoming, her bone marrow stopped protecting her. We suffered watching my mommy, my beautiful, loving, kind, selfless best friend die.

My world had crumbled, my heart was shattered, and my spirit was broken. I was catapulted into the role of 'mother' to my younger prepubescent brother, 'caretaker' to my elderly maternal grandparents, and Chief Operations Officer to my uncle's medical practice, where I had assumed my mother's position. Worst of all, I was left to communicate directly with my father.

I returned to the comfort of my familiar, exciting, and downright dysfunctional relationship. I needed to fill the gaping hole left by the loss of my mom, cloak the pain, and create a sense of home. I needed to feel loved again.

SHOUTS FROM THE ROOFTOP...PROTECT YOUR BROTHER!

At twenty-one years old, I had reached a critical turning point where the call demanded I protect my brother and, in doing so, dig deep to discover the depth and strength of my own spirit. I traded my independence, my burgeoning self expression, and fortified self-worth for duty. I rose to the occasion and found solace in my relationship.

With the loss of our biggest cheerleader and dependence upon my father's inability to parent growing worse, I needed all of the support I could garner. I protected my brother from his dangerous downward spiral, became his legal guardian, moved him out of my dad's home, and my husband provided him with a job in our business. I appreciated my love's love, and his efforts to support me, and my family, and soon married.

Motivated by my desire to understand why bad things happen to good people—like my mom, I found Rabbi Kushner's book with that exact title! Undoubtedly, the most influential teacher was my introduction to the work of Norman Vincent Peale, *The Power of Positive Thinking*, and his ministry at Marble Collegiate Church in NYC. My spiritual path was illuminated, my energy began to flow, and my spirit was on the mend. For the first time, I experienced comfort in knowing that psychology and communication could help me figure things out, whilst spirituality offered me the grace I needed. I quickly became a leader of the women's group. Deepening my faith, I accepted that I was home, seen, heard, loved.

What I didn't know was that I was on the precipice of having the most monumental spiritual breakthrough—our first child, a girl, my daughter, was born on my mommy's birthday. Divine breadcrumbs, indeed. I gave birth to my second daughter soon after, and life felt full and loving. Two perfectly healthy, beautiful angels, my daughters become the light of my life. Life was sweet and lighter than it had ever been. I wished it wouldn't end.

After several attempts, my husband created a baby of his own—a hedge fund with considerable responsibilities and financial obligations. Headquartered on Park Ave, the stakes were high, and the performance-driven nature of the business is not for the faint of heart. Caring for his baby took a different toll on him, his partners, and our family. Mental health cracks show and I thought it was temporary...I think once we have X amount under management, and X amount of employees, he will drink less, be more present, and be less angry. Or, I know, what if we moved across the country? I chose to ignore, push the awareness down, the warning signs, and take a leap of faith to look for a new home three-thousand miles away.

It was a period of intense accountability and at the same time, deep appreciation.

SHOUTING GROWS LOUDER TO DEAFENING SCREAMS...PROTECT YOUR DAUGHTERS!

At thirty years old, I found myself more at home, more aware and alive than I have ever felt. The stark contrast of the concrete jungle of my urban upbringing was cleansed by the most incredible natural beauty. I felt anchored to the powerful mountains and in flow with this magnificent body of water named Lake Tahoe. At first, I enjoyed the peace and quiet. The business was thriving and required a lot of his attention. Abundance flowed, Grandma was with us and healthy, and I loved being a mother as our children blossomed into incredible little people.

However, our dysfunctional marriage was now front and center. With no extended family dramas and no social engagements, I had to accept there was a huge elephant in the room. His argumentative narcissistic style was at the heart of our arguments. Often, he would go away for days without contact. I wondered if there was someone else. *Am I not good enough, smart enough, thin enough?*

I screamed at my reflection in the mirror, "I HATE my life!"

With no more than the blink of my eye, I yelled back, "No, you don't! You hate your situation!"

Choose differently and change everything. I had chosen to repeat the patterns my mom had modeled, despite all of the lessons bestowed upon me. Now I was responsible for shaping these young girls' well-being. I choose to get help.

This call was a deafening scream. I liken it to my two-by-four theory, one that involves a large plank of wood hitting you upside your head because you have been ignoring the plea. It's true what they say when you ignore something; it comes back in spades. It became crystal clear that the Universe demanded my attention. I am faced with the only choice I could imagine, I choose to protect my daughters.

After several drug-fueled psychotic breaks and numerous rehabilitation attempts, he is unable to stabilize and becomes dangerous to himself and others. I divorced him. Our family splintered, and soon after, reeled with grief from his subsequent suicide. I am alone, in pain, confused about who I am, what I am doing, and how to figure it all out.

I attended psychotherapy sessions twice a week and found that meditation, journaling, mindfulness, Reiki, energy work, and angel readings saved my sanity and held my heart open. I nurtured myself. I stayed positive. I practiced yoga and Pilates and grew strong and balanced. I connected my mind, and body to my spirit.

I also created and fostered a community of like-minded seekers who were authentic and lived in gratitude. I served my community. I loved my children. Full of pride, I exhaled, "I will love again and again and again."

A couple of years later I would meet my second husband in Tahoe, and we would begin to build a new home.

ONLY CALL THAT I ANSWER...PROTECT YOUR INNER PEACE.

The years that followed continued to challenge us, from financial devastation to the trials and tribulations of raising teenagers, painful grief, and step-parenting. The business that provided our security imploded at the exact time that the real estate market crashed in 2009. Having been directed by most experts, from lawyers to accountants, we were invested in the real estate market as a preventative measure from my ex-husband having access to large sums of cash. Aware that there was no way to keep the properties afloat, including our beloved home with views of Lake Tahoe, I accepted our fate. I cut the final chord of a long lost dream and released my children's childhood home. We headed south to the beaches of San Diego to create a new home and trusted that love would lead us to a peaceful path.

I was divinely nudged to contact an old high school friend who shared her work online to help others change their lives. She persuaded me to take what was then called, Creative Insight Journey Class, online. My mind was blown, my eyes opened, and my heart expanded. When I called her to express how meaningful and serendipitous this experience had become, she offered me the first opportunity to become a Clarity Catalyst coach and teach the course.

This call was a "Hell, yes!" and as they say, the rest is history.

These courses provided a framework for me to share my mind, body, and spirit connection with my love, my children, my friends and family. It's a "practical playbook" to live your life to its fullest and has changed my life. I credit my coaching and training that gave me the ability to allow my life to unfold by saying a hearty 'yes' to opportunity and letting go of the 'how'.

My life is full of adventure as I split my time between the desert and the mountains of California. We visit Lake Tahoe often, spending time with our daughters and those in our beautiful community who still reside there. My sense of home has expanded, and I no longer need to be somewhere to feel at home. That feeling resides in me. I am always home.

My husband and I grow daily in our intimacy as we continue to embark upon a conscious journey inward together, deepening our love and devotion to one another. My daughters are smart, creative, confident women living in their authenticity. Our communication thrives at the center of all of our relationships, and even when we falter, we rely on the notion that we will love each other again. I choose love and appreciate all that we have been through.

Life often teaches us that our experiences and circumstances shape us, molding our perspectives and dictating our actions. However, true transformation begins when we shift our focus inward. By exploring our inner world, we redefine our understanding of the external world on our terms.

This shift from external blame to internal responsibility is the essence of "calling you in, not out." It is about becoming aware and embracing our thoughts, preferences, feelings, beliefs, and actions with radical acceptance, accountability, and appreciation.

Four

Finding Grace

Penning the Path to Healing and Hope

JENNIFER GRACE

It was 4 a.m., and I was writing, producing, and directing the 2015 horror movie starring me. In this movie, I was cast as the mother who had lost her son...forever.

It had been one week, two days, three hours, and forty-seven minutes since my fourteen-year-old son had left my house and had not come back.

It had been three weeks of hell prior to that exiting.

My sweet baby boy had suddenly turned into the devil incarnate. Between starting high school, feeling overwhelmed by his new school workload, hormones raging, and feeling frustrated that we did not live near any of his friends in our new neighborhood, my fifteen-year-old son began to rage.

Except now he was three inches taller than me.

Chairs would get turned over. Flash cards would fly when I asked him to finish his homework.

A fury of curse words would spill out of his mouth when I would say, "Dinner is ready, sweetie."

And finally, he got up in my face, grabbed my arms, and pushed me when I told him it was time for bed at almost half-past midnight. "You can't tell me what to do. I hate you and I hate this f-ing house."

Anyone who has a teenager ever experienced this? Anyone?

I called his dad. We had been divorced for eight years and had a strong friendship and a good co-parenting relationship.

The next day, after making a joint decision, Cole went to live across town with his father.

It was September 11; I kid you not.

The first four nights, I downed a bottle of chardonnay and passed out watching *Hollywood Housewives*. It always makes me feel better about my own life when I get to watch someone else's more pathetic life. Yes, I know that sounded judgmental, but it's true.

On the morning of the fifth day, I knew that waking up with a dry mouth and a pounding head was not serving myself, my boyfriend, Sev, my students, nor my clients. I had to find another way of dealing with this pain.

I remembered a quote I read once by Jon Kabat-Zinn when I studied Buddhism. I found it in a book and read it aloud to myself.

"Because there are no drugs that will make you immune to stress or pain or that will magically solve your problems. It will take conscious effort on your part to move in the direction of healing and peace. This means learning to work with the very stress and pain that is causing you to suffer."

Did he just say learning to work with the very stress and pain that is causing you to suffer?

Fantastic, Jon. Sounds like a party.

I wanted to crawl out of my skin. I didn't want to be me. I didn't want to be a mother who had lost her son.

On the way to my bedroom on that fifth night, sober as hell, I opened the door to his bedroom, which I had kept shut since he left.

Falling to my knees onto the floor, I crumbled into a sobbing mess. *I bet this is what a mother must feel like when her son dies*, I thought.

I rocked and cried on that floor, for what seemed like eternity, for myself and for all those heartbroken mothers.

I missed my sweet boy so much. We had been thick as thieves for fifteen years, and now he had walked out and left me like some jilted lover.

I crawled into bed and tried to sleep.

Since the sobbing had exhausted me, I fell right out that night. But at 4 a.m., like every single night, I woke up to the horror movie that would play out in my mind until the sun came up—the one where I would never have a relationship with my son again.

Then finally at 6 a.m., I would rise, busy myself with work during the day and TV at night, which were simply other forms of chardonnay, and try to pretend I was, "learning to work with the very stress and pain that was causing me to suffer."

Who exactly was I trying to kid?

FINDING GRACE

Is that 100% going to happen, Jen?

The voice jolted me out of the movie theater of my mind.

The familiar scene had been running—the one where I was old and gray, dying in a hospital, and my son had not once come to visit me. I looked around my bedroom. My boyfriend was sound asleep, and of course, looking at my phone, it was 4 horror o'clock in the morning again.

I heard the voice again: *Is that 100% going to happen, Jen?*

"Is what going to happen?" I said this aloud in a harsh whisper.

That. That scene you keep playing over and over in your mind, where you never see Cole again and you die miserable and alone?

The voice was very peaceful and calm.

I suddenly realized the voice was coming from deep inside me.

I froze. Who was this voice?

I decided I should ask, *um, who are you?*

It's Grace.

Grace?

So, are you going to answer me or not? Is this scene in your mind that you keep playing out, 100% beyond a shadow of a doubt, going to happen?

Well, I guess I don't really know. It might.

And…it might not.

Well, yes, that's true.

Why do you hold onto the thought that it will when that clearly causes you to suffer, and it may not even turn out to be true?

Because I can't help myself.

You can't or you won't?

I don't know.

What if you focused on the thought that this is part of your growing and learning process while you are here attending this school called earth? That this turn of events is bringing you rich wisdom and truth? That this tumultuous time is gifting you with finally getting to meet me?

Who are you, anyway?

Why, I'm your consciousness.

I'm the part of you who will always live and never die. I am your awareness. I am your essence. For lack of a better term, I am your soul.

Wow. Holy shit. Um, well, it's nice to meet you then. I have a future self named Grace, too. Are you the same Grace?

She ignored the last question and continued, *Jen, I am the one who can interrupt you when you start to suffer. I am the one who can ask you powerful questions and get you to see the truth. I am the one who will always remain calm, responsive, non-reactive, non-judgmental. I am clear, grounded, wise, and ready at any moment to help you regain your balance.*

Well then, it is a pleasure to meet you, Grace!

I would love to say the same, Jen, yet I have known you all your lives.

That was the day I met Grace—my awareness, my audience, my soul.

WRITING THROUGH THE PAIN

I avoided my journal like the plague when Cole left. I did not want to write the words *Cole is gone* onto a blank page because if I did, I would be forced to accept the truth of it.

In the first few weeks, I was in a state of distracted denial, and I was quite happy there. The pain was so severe; I needed my buffers of *Hollywood Housewife* marathons, my chardonnay (I make progress, I was down from a bottle to two glasses a night), and getting lost in my current novel that I was revisiting, *The Diary of Anne Frank*.

As the sharpness of the pain began to subside by using my mindfulness tools, my serotonin had increased, which in turn decreased my stress and anxiety. I suddenly felt ready to face the page.

Writing takes great courage.

When I teach my transformational eight-week course, I ask my students to partake in a daily practice of ten minutes of meditation a day and five minutes of journaling.

The journaling type I prescribe is called porthole writing.

There is a time between sleep and wake that Einstein and Thomas Edison knew about, and it's called the Twilight State.

What Edison used to do was fall asleep sitting in a chair with a fork in his hand and a metal plate under him. When he would doze off and fall asleep, the fork would hit the pan and wake him up. In this moment, he discovered many of his brilliant inventions.

So, I ask my students to put a journal by their nightstand, and the moment they wake up, put pen to paper and write in a stream of consciousness for five timed minutes every day.

I warn them that this is a practice, and they should not be surprised if they don't "discover electricity" during their first journaling session because, well, it's already been discovered. But if they come to this practice every single day, eventually they will tap into the wisdom of themselves as well as universal wisdom.

A "porthole" will open, and they will access their deep wells of creativity.

Sounds profound and quite enrolling, right?

About thirty-five percent of them never do it.

Why?

They are scared shitless.

I told you; writing takes courage.

Until you can face the truth, you will continue to do what you do—distracting and dancing as fast as you can to the tune of: Show binging, spending hours on social media, counseling countless friends about their problems, overworking, over-drinking, overeating. You get the picture. We all do it. Until we don't.

These are all painkillers. Except they don't kill the pain—they only mask it.

Finally, I was ready to face my truth.

I opened my journal, half expecting dust and cobwebs to fly out. It felt so long since I had written.

I picked up my favorite pen and I wrote the first line:

Cole is gone.

Then I dropped the pen and cried for a solid three minutes. Then, I wrote my next few lines.

I am utterly embarrassed. What kind of transformational trainer loses her son? I teach others how to use mindfulness to create peace and harmony in their lives, and my own son hates me? I feel so disgusted with myself. I want to crawl out of my skin. I want to move to another city where no one knows my name. I am so ashamed.

Why did he leave me? Why does he hate me? What did I do?

I think maybe I need to tell some of my friends. I mean, my friends are all professional therapists and coaches! Maybe they have some insight, some wisdom. Maybe I need to get support. Maybe this is normal for teenage boys to do this; maybe he wanted to just go live with his dad. I don't know what to think. I need help. I think I should call Deb.

The rambling, the embarrassment, and the shame I allowed myself to pour onto that page led me to clarity, as it always does.

Deb was a dear friend of mine who was a licensed therapist, and she was the first person besides my partner, Sev, I finally told.

She was so wonderful and sent me two things: The first was an article from *Psychology Today* speaking about the dynamic of mother and son during the coming of age and puberty years, and the second was a poem.

The article explained that when teenage boys hit puberty and begin to become sexually attracted to girls, they often want to detach from their mothers.

This article went on to say if they were from a divorced family, they would also feel the need to be more in the presence of the male figure in their life. They need more male role modeling and less coddling from their mother. It is common that they will for a time completely reject their mother.

Okay, I thought. This is normal.

I'm not crazy.

The poem she sent me was written by a teenage son to his mother. It was a beautiful poem, but it was this line that stayed with me:

"Mama, before I go out into the world, I will first have to sharpen my claws on you."

And that is exactly what he had done. He had taken all his bottled-up rage, confused hormones, and the anger many teenagers experience, and poured it out all over me. Why? Because he knew I could take it. And he knew I would still love him unconditionally.

He couldn't let it out at school; he would be expelled, and his father certainly would have not tolerated that sort of behavior.

He let it out on me because somewhere underneath all that teenage rage, he trusted me.

And he was right to.

That journal entry I had prolonged and procrastinated over for so many weeks turned out to be my saving grace. If I had not put pen to paper that morning, I would have never gotten the clarity to call Deb. That article and poem became an invitation to now belong to a tribe of mothers who were not abusers and were not crack addicts—they were just like me. Women who had taken one for the team as their sons made their rite of passage from boys to men.

I also would have kept blaming and shaming myself, instead of holding a strong intention that this was normal, and that my son would come home when he was ready, and we would have the opportunity to resume a good healthy mother son relationship.

Six months later, almost to the day, he came home.

Since then, we have been thick as thieves. Like it never even happened.

So, write.

Write through the confusion to get to the clarity.

Write through the pain to get to peace.

Write through the avoidance to get to the acceptance.

Just write.

Five

Playing the Long Game

Building Your Castle One Brick at a Time

TONI NAPOLITANO

I was laid out flat on my back on the white couch in my stylish downtown Miami high-rise apartment, staring at the ceiling thanks to a not-so-stylish medical grade neck brace. I was listening to the TV (turning my head was not an option) and feeling guilty for being unproductive, but also feeling like I could breathe for the first time in forever.

I had been working for a luxury fashion house, once a dream come true, that in recent years had ebbed into more of a nightmare. The expectation to deliver ever-increasing results was all consuming. My most well respected peer confided that she was taking Klonopin to deal with the pressure. I wondered how many others were doing the same. I knew I was miserable but weren't most people in their jobs? And mine was more glam than most.

Wasn't this the life I'd worked for? Didn't I have what I, what everyone, wanted? My sky-high stress level whispered that I didn't, but I pretended not to notice.

As my dad often reminded me, "They don't pay you for nothing kid!" But when we don't give heed to the whisper, it has a way of starting to shout.

Fate threw me a lifeline disguised as three herniated discs. Placed on a spiritual timeout, I was forced to be still, to get present with my own thoughts. To rest. I started to hear the small voice inside me again, the one I thought had disappeared, but our voice of wisdom never truly leaves. She was just waiting patiently for me to get quiet enough to listen.

As I lay there immobile and bored, a sudden picture of my college roommate, Sally, who I hadn't seen in years, popped into my head. Something nudged me to reach out. She responded immediately, happy to hear from me, and we began to close the gap on what we'd been up to. She was currently living in Dubai building a tech start up and was attending a retreat in Venice, Italy.

"Why don't you join me? It's like meeting in the middle for both of us!" she said.

It was called Creative Rehab, a week-long container for reconnecting with and healing your childlike creative spirit. In Venice. It sounded perfect! I clicked the link and signed up.

Looking back, something awoke in me in Venice, at least that is when my first big domino fell. On this retreat, surrounded by my friend and ten other brilliant companions from all over the world, I began to question everything I thought I knew.

I allowed myself to admit I was unhappy. I knew I didn't want to keep going the way I was. Stumbling through each day trying to finish a ridiculous to do list of someone else's expectations, which was ever growing and never ending. I was existing, marking time till the salvation of each next day off or vacation and trying my best not to fail. I was living with, walking with, sleeping with, and eating with **fear** as my constant companion. I was going through the motions and felt paralyzed, clinging to a routine that was slowly killing me. I should have run, but I was so accustomed to the mind-numbing exhaustion, I couldn't conceive possibilities outside my immediate line of sight and survival.

I had to come clean. I was a work junkie who didn't know how to stop. I knew it wasn't healthy, but I was terrified of change. Afraid if I let go, even for an instant, that everything would fall apart. The mental and emotional pattern, the need to be needed, ran so deep I had no idea it was driving every choice, action, and decision.

My drug of choice was not only socially acceptable, it was highly respected, applauded even.

"She's so dedicated!" "Such a hard worker!" my friends and family would say with pride each time I missed a gathering, holiday, or milestone event.

Everyone envied my "glamorous" life. But I was losing sight of who I was. Feeling myself drift further away from the creativity and joy that drew me to fashion in the first place.

It's amazing what happens when you surround yourself with a different group of people. In my world, everyone was existing as I was, so we all thought it was normal. Now I was having conversations with people who were seekers, willing to get uncomfortable on the journey of self discovery. Between immersion in the beauty of Venice, great conversation and company, and workshops that felt more like intense therapy sessions, I was finally feeding my heart and soul what I didn't realize it was starving from.

At our closing ceremony, we wrote down what we were committed to change to live the life of our dreams, and then each person would walk to the front of the room, declaring it to the group and throwing it into the fire. This was accountability! Shaking in my designer boots, I shuffled towards the moment of truth, equal parts terrified and exhilarated. I stepped up to the smiling moderator, held up my paper, and boldly declared, "I'm quitting my job!"

The room went wild as I watched my paper float down into the silver bucket of our makeshift fire pit and disappear into smoke. I had never felt so supported! I knew in my heart this was right; it was a full body *yes*, but my mind had no idea how I was going to pull it off.

The thing about big decisions is we think that the earth under our feet will shift the minute we make them. It's a bit anticlimactic when it feels like a small tremor instead of a massive quake. The truth is it's much bigger, too big to process in real time. It's the entire universe that's shifting. But we don't yet have that wider scope of vision to connect the dots and see the intricate web of magic at play. We are focused on the here and now while the universe plays the long game.

Back home, away from the supportive retreat community, the reactions I received were less than enthusiastic and ran the gamut from skeptical to outright questioning my sanity.

I told myself that if I couldn't figure things out in a year, I could return to a corporate role. I had a strong track record and a great network. I felt confident in my safety-net ability to get a position if I needed one. I was just as confident that I would never need to exercise that option. I believed that given time and space, the perfect solution would present itself. I had no idea what I wanted to do. Only a vague awareness that I wanted to tap into my spiritual gifts, do something that made me feel happy and fulfilled, and where I got to help other people feel the same way.

Imagine my surprise when twelve months later, my happiness fund was running low, and I was no closer (or so it seemed) to an answer. I thought about all the incredible and life-changing experiences I had in the past year. I went to therapy for the first time. This allowed the painful memories of childhood abuse to resurface and I began to heal from them. I started a daily meditation practice and did yoga. I was proud of the progress I had made!

I traveled to Bali for a second Creative Rehab retreat, to Australia to see koalas, and to sun-drenched Nicaragua for a yoga intensive. I met new people who lit my soul up! I made time to reconnect with friends and family I had lost touch with during my hectic work days. I started to regulate my nervous system.

It felt like a long undoing process to get back to center. I read books, went to concerts, attended lectures, met friends for coffee, and spent hours discussing philosophy and quantum physics. I volunteered at a monthly yoga event that raised money for charity, and at a local halfway house that helped families. I was peaceful, happy, and fulfilled.

However, I was also starting to panic about how to pay the bills. Has the Universe let me down? Where was my perfect spiritually fulfilling vocation? Still partially anchored to my old conditioning, I surmised that one year off would be sufficient time to heal my childhood wounds, decide what I wanted to do with the rest of my life, and build that unknown but brilliant and successful business. Where had I gone wrong?

I prayed for guidance. What I got was a constant pop up for about a week on my social media channels for a lecture at a local cafe by Hay House author Jennifer Grace. She was teaching how to *Drop the Rope*, her book about letting go of stress at will. I signed up.

After the interactive lecture, Jennifer shared that she was teaching a class called Creative Insight Journey (CIJ), an eight-week program to help you get clear on your life's purpose. Bingo! Once again I followed the breadcrumbs, certain that *this was it*. At the end of eight weeks, I would *know*.

Four weeks in, I had to admit I was learning a lot, making friends with even more women who inspired me, and while I was healing generational trauma, I still had no idea what I wanted to do. I had to make a decision. My financial situation was getting sticky.

While I wasn't worried about finding another job, I was crestfallen that I needed one. I received a dream offer to work with a prestigious brand I had always admired. Exactly what I'd done prior, same job, different company. They were willing to match my salary and all the benefits of the role I had previously left. I would make a generous income with a clothing allowance, and all of my travel expenses covered.

Most people would be thrilled. I was appreciative of the arrival of this gift just when I needed it, yet I also felt like a giant failure. I was frustrated with myself for not finding the answer. Shouldn't I know my own dream by now? I hadn't gone after this job, it had found me. It all lined up so easily that I knew it must be the right thing, but I also felt like I was taking the easy way out. I was giving up, going back to the industry I had just escaped. I had no way of knowing what was just around the corner.

I took a leap of faith, and could feel my excitement start to build as I envisioned bringing my newly grounded and balanced self to the table. In this mindset, what kind of transformation could I inspire? Maybe I could become a catalyst for radical change in the industry! Same job, new me...what if I was the difference?

The first year flew by, but once the honeymoon phase wore off, it was clear that the industry hadn't changed just because I did. It was still brutal. Despite the vastness of my optimism, one person can't change an entire industry, at least not quickly, yet somehow I was exactly where I needed to be.

Who could have foreseen the Covid-19 pandemic and lock-down? Suddenly an entire employee population was sitting at home paid. We were totally unprepared to keep them both busy and supported. My boss asked for suggestions. I boldly submitted CIJ and speed dialed Jen, with my voice bursting with excitement. She was on board!

This traditional and conservative company would never have entertained an expenditure on mindfulness training under normal circumstances. This was a golden opportunity to introduce transformative tools to people in desperate need. I loved this industry that had given me so much and wanted to do everything I could to help it heal from the inherent toxicity.

I would like to tell you everything changed, but that's not entirely true. I changed. I spoke my mind, stood my ground and set boundaries. I reclaimed myself! I met incredible people who I love to this day. I started to collect other puzzle shapes and piece them together. I may not have reformed the entire company or industry culture, but I started a ripple. Every person our class touched will carry that forward into their work and lives. When you're playing the long game, a ripple can become a tsunami.

It took a few years to get clear on my dream of helping other strong women recover from burnout and infusing mindfulness into corporate culture. I needed to heal first. I learned that the greatest impact we can make is on ourselves. Now I help others do that, too. After all, you can't lead someone to someplace you've never been.

I also learned that to find my soulmate, I needed to listen to my soul. When I started doing what made me happy instead of what I *should* do, doors began to open like never before. I went on a Wine, Women, and Yoga retreat in California with Jennifer; just because it sounded fun, and ended up meeting the love of my life.

Time and perspective provide great clarity around our challenges. Something that has helped me connect the dots is an exercise I call Look for the Long Game.

I use a mind map template and think about a past challenging situation. I give it a name (ex. Neck Injury), and I write it in the center circle. Setting five minutes on a timer, I let it play out like a movie in my head, from where I was then to where I am now. I fill in each smaller circle with a ripple from the situation. People I met as a result, places I went, things I experienced. No matter how small, things that came out of that situation that might not have happened otherwise. Where did each one of them lead me? I continue to fill in as many circles as I can.

Reverse reviewing the chain of events, I start to comprehend the connections that did not seem important at the time, and all the synchronicities they have led to. It's mind blowing to realize how the threads are connected and how interwoven and perfectly orchestrated every action is.

The biggest lesson I took away is that the big picture doesn't reveal itself on our timeline; it has a mind of its own. In the moment, we can't always grasp the perspective to see it. As I look back now, I can connect with brilliant clarity the importance of each step, how they all were part of the bigger dance. I started my journey expecting to see my dream on the horizon like a beautiful shining castle, something I could trek towards, never realizing that with each step I was creating it from inside myself, the Universe handing me one brick at a time.

Six

For a Greater Purpose

How I Used My Second Chance at
Life to Advocate for Others

DANETTE BROWN

I t was supposed to be the summer of new beginnings, a summer full of excitement and promise for my two roommates and I. I was eighteen years old and had not been out on my own for long, but I was ready to take on a new adventure with the two girlfriends I had come to know and trust. We were thrilled to move to the big city, well at least it was our state's big city. We already found an apartment adequate for the three of us, and since we all worked at the same place, we were able to transfer our positions to our new hometown.

Three days before our move, I arrived home around 9:30 p.m. One of my roommates was home. Feeling exhausted, I got into my comfy pjs, propped myself up on a fluffy pillow on my bed, and invited my roomie to join me as I could sense her eagerness to talk. I received an unexpected second wind from our combined excitement about our upcoming move. We shared our hopes and dreams and how we envisioned our new life. About an hour-and-a-half later, with our conversation winding down, my eyelids heavy, and my body sinking further into my bed, it was apparent my second wind lost the air in its sails, and I was ready to sleep.

My roommate attempted to lure me to join her in picking up our other roommate who was at work. Without hesitation, I protested. There was one thing, and one thing only on my agenda, and that was sleep!

In between the soft, cool sheets and rhythmic feel of my waterbed, I fell into a deep sleep. The next thing I remember is coming out of this coma-like state awakened by the overhead light, and trying to make sense of what my eyes were seeing.

As the sleep gave way, a male figure in front of and above me came into focus. With the horrifying realization that an intruder was straddling me, out of desperation and instinct I swung my left arm and hit him below his shoulder. I knew I had to knock him off me and run! I knocked him off me as my blankets became like gnarled vines keeping my legs entangled, and I struggled to gain my balance and momentum. Getting out of my waterbed proved to be an impossible challenge. My attempt to run was unsuccessful.

The intruder regained his straddling position as I braced myself sitting up with my legs extended out in front of me. A hundred thoughts raced through my mind still trying to make sense of what was happening. With my heart pounding, I told myself over and over again, *Breathe, stay calm, if you're calm, you'll get through this.*

To my surprise the intruder uttered no words, did not lay a hand on me, but instead went straight for the jewelry box I had on my headboard. With my senses fully awake, my nose took in the pungent smell of hard liquor in his breath; my eyes could see my watch he discovered in the jewelry box clenched between his teeth.

His focus remained on the items on my headboard. He had not spoken to me and had not shown any signs of violence. I began to think, *He wasn't there to hurt me; he was there to steal from me.*

In an instant, the thought shattered as he pulled a gun directly to my chest, and for the first time demanded money. My instincts sent my body into a protective, almost fetal, posture as my chest muscles tightened. My heart felt as though it stopped in anticipation of feeling the impact of the bullet. I was able to utter the words, "I don't have any money." to which he replied, "Well shut up or I will shoot you!" I complied, trying to keep from hyperventilating. I repeated over and over in my head, *Breathe, stay calm, you'll get through this.*

I knew he had put the gun down somewhere because I could see both of his hands holding the jewelry box again. Another sigh of relief overcame me as I thought, *He was only trying to scare you. If he were going to hurt you, he would have shot you.*

Just then he grabbed me by my left arm, turned me down on the bed, and with the cold metal of the gun shoved against the back of my neck, he fired one time. I had no doubt I was shot. The heat of the bullet felt as though a cigarette was burning a pathway through my neck. The smell of gunpowder was suffocating as it filled the entire room. I could see the wall and carpet as I lay on my bed. I knew I had been hit in the neck, the head, somewhere vital. It was at that point I anticipated death.

Accepting this fate, I closed my eyes expecting to be among the clouds arriving at Heaven's gate. I opened my eyes minutes later only to see the wall and the carpet. I opened and closed my eyes numerous times, realizing I hadn't gone anywhere. *Lord, why am I still here?*

I reached for the back of my neck and gasped as my entire palm was now red with blood. I realized that I was not going to die, at least not right then; I knew I needed to get help. I rolled off the bed and pounded on the block wall yelling, "Call the police, call the police!" hoping my elderly neighbor heard me.

As I walked out of my bedroom into my roommate's bedroom, my head bent downwards, I was holding my bleeding neck and crying. As I took a few steps into her room, there the intruder stood at the end of her bed rifling through items he had dumped out from one of her packed boxes. A glint caught my eye in the unlit room and upon a closer look, I realized it was the gun next to his right hand. If I ran through the bedroom and into the living room, my only way out of the apartment, he could shoot me in the back. We were in such proximity to each other due to the small size of the room; this encounter was unavoidable. Through tears I begged him not to hurt me again.

Not taking any chances, I reached across his body to place my hand over the gun so he would not aim it at me. Shocked by his hand running up my leg, I thought, *No, this is not happening!*

At that moment I lifted my knee and went for his groin. It was not the direct hit I aimed or hoped for, but his body bent down in a protective position, and it was enough to get his attention. Next, he ran for the living room door. Without thinking I chased behind him, placing my bloody palm print on the open front door, my other hand pushed against his back, and he took off running.

With the adrenaline rushing through my body, I ran next door, pounding on the door yelling, "It's Danette, help me, help me, I am hurt!"

My elderly neighbor had terror in her eyes and dialed 911. As I waited for the ambulance, I caught a glimpse of myself in a full-length mirror and winced as my face appeared as though someone had taken their finger and shoved it through my cheek. This was the event that changed the course of my life.

FROM SURVIVAL TO SERVICE

The X-rays and CT scans revealed I was shot in the back of the neck/base of the skull on the left side of my head. The bullet hit the C2 vertebrae, traveled all the way around the back of my neck, and lodged in my right jaw. Now I knew why my face looked like it had a finger shoved into it. Several times the doctors scheduled surgery, but after consultations with specialists we decided it was best to leave the bullet in its location rather than risk paralyzing my face.

One neurologist often called me his "good luck charm" stating he could not explain why I'm here. Had the bullet gone millimeters in any direction, it would have resulted in either certain death or paralysis from the neck down. For me, there was only one explanation–God.

Although the nightmare of that night ended with the intruder fleeing my home, what would come as a result was just the beginning. The physical, mental, and emotional impact emerged. I could not wash my hair without being in excruciating pain. The weight of the water would bring tears to my eyes as my face turned beet red. Simple motions of bending my neck forward caused sensations of shocking electricity running up and down my back on either side. Nighttime had become my adversary, and fear and anxiety accompanied darkness like a child's fear of the boogeyman. I was glad to live under my parent's roof again because I felt safe in my dad's presence. However, severe insomnia would become an unwelcome antagonist for most of my adult life.

The next months and years entailed dealings with the criminal justice system–mugshot books, lineups, and having to face the intruder in court. After some time had passed, I worked in the prosecutor's office that oversaw my case. It was there that I experienced the workings of the criminal justice system. I was already a proponent of law enforcement as the detectives on my case were so good to me.

Years later I decided to go to college to become a psychologist who would help victims overcome the tragic events they experienced. As part of my curriculum, I took an elective course entitled Victimology in the Criminal Justice Department. The course viewed the criminal justice system from the victim's perspective. That course sparked my interest in law enforcement. After obtaining my bachelor's degree in psychology, I pursued a master's degree in criminal justice.

My degrees led me to an incredible and fulfilling career in law enforcement. I retired after twenty-five years of service as a civilian Investigator Supervisor where I led our Investigation Bureau's Intelligence Unit for twenty-four of my twenty-five years. The event that could have ended my life fueled my passion to fight for justice for victims and their families. It was important to me that victims were not forgotten, their lives mattered, and we would do our part to hold their assailants responsible. My position not only entailed working and overseeing criminal investigations, but also providing leadership, guidance, and mentoring my team both in their professional and personal lives.

As I contemplated retirement, it was important to continue to serve others. In addition to surviving the shooting, my journey also included broken relationships and divorce. One breakup in particular left me doubting my ability to make decisions, beating myself up for not seeing it coming, and wondering how I was so wrong about this person. It was one of the most challenging times in my life.

After reflecting on my past experiences, I decided to become a certified life coach who specializes in empowering women. As part of my coaching career, I guide women who have experienced trauma through their own healing journey. I also use my past experience to offer personal safety workshops, and I collaborate with a company to teach self-defense classes, so women can take responsibility for their own personal security. Law enforcement functions from a reactive standpoint, meaning that a crime has already been committed against a person. These workshops and classes are intended to raise awareness and provide tools to help women and prevent them from becoming victimized in the first place.

When horrible things happen, we cannot help but question, *Why? Why did this happen? Why me?*

I have come to accept there are many questions I will never know the answers to on this side of Heaven. For me, I had to ask myself, *Where are you going to expend your limited time and energy?*

We can replay, over-analyze, dissect what has happened to us, but it does not change the outcome. Even if we receive some answers, I have found that most of the time they're never satisfactory because we are trying to make sense of what is senseless. As part of your healing journey, you can ask yourself questions, including:

What can I learn from this situation about myself, others, and events that happen beyond my control?

How can I use this situation to experience personal and spiritual growth?

How can I use what happened to me to help others?

LEARN TO FORGIVE

Forgiveness. Now this is a difficult but vital part of healing. It rarely comes naturally, or without God's strength, but without forgiveness, true healing is not possible. We must learn to forgive ourselves from the doubts, self-blame, and what ifs that often fill our minds. If we do not learn to let go, we allow the events that happened to us to become what defines us and live as prisoners of our past.

Often the most challenging part is forgiving the offender who hurt us. I forgave the intruder years ago. I do not know his story. I do not know what led him to the point where he was willing to take a life–my life–for a few items of such little value. What I do know and believe with all my being is that God had other plans for my life. Plans to be of service to others.

What I have learned through life-altering events is they become part of who you are, part of your story, because they impact our lives in such a profound way. We have no control over when or why they happen, but we do have control of how they affect our lives.

When asked how I got through such a horrific event at such an early age, my answer is simple: faith, purpose, and persistence. There were times when I loathed the dark, so I would light a candle and watch the flickering light. For me, it was a visual representation.

No matter how dark life felt, God's presence was with me piercing through the darkness. He would light and direct my path. In the end everything that happened to me, and will happen to me, has been and will be for a greater purpose—His.

Seven

Love Heals All

Moving from Pain to Purpose

AARON MASTNY

Sometimes things don't make sense until they do. Why is this? Well, what if my subconscious mind blocks me from accessing the part of me that could bring forth the highest version of who I am in this moment? Not because my subconscious is bad, but because it got programmed a long time ago to protect me from the pain I experienced as a child.

A lot of coaching tells you to forget the past and just focus on getting results. Some therapies are focused on digging up your past to help resolve those issues in our minds. Then you have the meditation and Buddhism movement, which tells you to be here now. What if the answer to our happiness, joy, peace, love, self empowerment, and freedom was a combination of all of these modalities?

What if the problem was that we were never taught the game of life and how it works, which causes us to do things in a certain sequence that only creates more of what we don't want?

I can give you all the right ingredients to bake a cake, but if you don't put them in the right order, you don't get what you want.

There are certain universal laws that when we abide by them the cosmic energy of creation works in our favor and puts us in the rhythm of life. Some call this a flow state, but the real question is, *How do I learn these universal laws and apply them in such a way where I can express my authentic self?*

In my experience, most of us have been conditioned to stay in fight, flight, and freeze. A lot of times it doesn't matter how hard you work, or the amount of money in your bank account, if you are doing things from a state of survival and scarcity you will never be enough.

There are also core limiting beliefs we all have that we have embodied since we were kids. This keeps us stuck in our unconscious self-sabotaging behaviors of pain, blame, and shame.

Carl Jung said, "Until we make the unconscious conscious, it will direct your life and you will call it fate. I am not what happened to me, I am what I choose to become."

We are all going through an ascension process, and every time we look to grow we hit our next unconscious block that prevents us from stepping into our next level. This applies to our bodies, relationships, and making money.

Over the last ten years I have spent thousands of hours helping my clients resolve generational trauma by reprogramming unconscious patterns of the past and processing uncomfortable emotions. The reason I'm so passionate about supporting people with this process is because I have walked through the valley of death and realized there was no way to run or hide from it.

By the time I was fourteen, I was binge drinking with my friends and addicted to feeling good. When I was nineteen I found heroin and made it my medicine to numb the childhood trauma I was holding in my body from a very young age. By twenty-three I was shooting heroin and got to the point where I thought I should exit this life for good.

For anyone who has ever felt suicidal, you understand that it's not a great place to be. At the time, I really didn't understand what was happening and why I was so depressed and shut down. I couldn't talk to anyone and I was scared to leave my apartment. I felt helpless, hopeless, numb, dissociated, checked out, and in a complete state of freeze. My mind was foggy, and as I continued to shoot heroin I felt dead inside.

At one point it got so bad that I chose to shoot heroin behind my girlfriend's back with her brother, Mark. She would find him nodding off on the couch and declare to the world, "He's going to fucking die!"

I was in a dark place with no hope in sight, so when my girlfriend's brother came to me and asked, "What should I do?"

I replied, "You need to get the fuck out of here!"

The thought was Mark would move to Salt Lake City and live where his dad was. Mark and Geneva were both brought up Mormon and I had been raised in a structured Bible fellowship group.

At that time my interpretation of God while growing up was that God loved me when I obeyed the Bible, and when I didn't, I was bad and wrong. This type of environment set me up for a tremendous amount of guilt, shame, and pain in the name of God.

Mark's mom helped him relocate out to Salt Lake. A week later she returned back to Philadelphia and told us, "Something was not right. Mark's spirit came to me the night before and said goodbye."

Not believing what I was hearing, we immediately reached out to the dad to check on Mark.

When their dad went by Mark's apartment there was no answer. When he came back the next morning and saw Mark's truck in the same spot, he called the cops.

When the police arrived they broke down the door and found Mark laid out on the couch with a needle in his arm. His body was discolored and everyone immediately knew he had been dead for a period of time.

At that moment the worst thing that could have ever happened just showed up. I was in complete disbelief and shock from the news being relayed to us over the phone.

The amount of sorrow and grief that followed this situation was unbearable. The only way I could survive was to do my best to acknowledge what was happening in a dissociated state. Since Mark was brought up Mormon by his mom and dad, most of the family was in Salt Lake City to meet us under the most intense set of circumstances.

Everyone was in shock. While most of the women mourned and cried, the men stood by stoically with anger and rage, blaming Mark for the selfish act he had chosen to do.

When Mark's mom and dad asked me to speak at the service because they didn't know what to say, I put myself into a deeper state of shut down. The reality was that I had just been shooting heroin with Mark right before he left to get help. I was holding in a secret that no one else knew, but Mark. I was the one who told Mark he should move out to Salt Lake, and *now he was fucking dead!* I believed it was my fault he was no longer here.

So many thoughts, feelings, and emotions ran through my body. Mark had been playing Russian roulette with his life since he was fourteen years old when he was first introduced to heroin. He discovered it when a local drug dealer offered it to him when his parents got divorced. This would be a recipe for the deeper pain that followed.

What the fuck do I say?! to a group of Mormon's who just lost their grandson, cousin, nephew, brother, and son. It was the ultimate nightmare of a family reunion and at some point all eyes would be on me to share something to make sense of something that I had no idea how to explain.

But before this would happen, we had the gruesome task of still having to identify my best friend in the morgue.

I remember walking downstairs into the dimly lit space where I saw Mark's body laid out on a table. His face was discolored and you could see his veins had turned green and purple because he had decomposed. I also recall the strong odor of death and decay that filled the air. As I stood there, I realized something for the first time in my twenty-three years of being on this planet. I saw my buddy's body as a suit. Although his body was there I recognized his spirit was not. It struck me hard and deep that wherever Mark had gone he was no longer in that body.

This lesson of I am a spirit having an experience through this body would become my life's work.

If you study the hypnotherapist Dr. George Pratt, you will learn he had over forty-five thousand clients who all had some version of these seven core limiting beliefs. I am not enough or I am worthless, I am not safe, I am not lovable, I am powerless, I am bad, I don't trust, I am alone.

I found that these core limiting beliefs are reflected back from our parents. From the time we are born until seven years old we are in a hypnotic theta brainwave state. We end up embodying these limiting beliefs anytime we didn't feel love or safety as a child and make these thoughts our identity. We then continuously reinforce this experience of pain. Then our mind tries to help us get us away from this pain and our unconscious mental habits are formed. This is what drove me to become a heroin addict because of the deep sexual trauma I experienced as a child.

When I was in third grade I was bullied for being one of the only Asian kids in an all-white school in the pine barrens of New Jersey. When I made my first friend; he was sexual towards me. This created a lot of confusion. Because I was brought up in a religious context that homosexuality was bad and wrong, I would hold onto this secret with shame. I then created a belief that God didn't love me because of what I had done. I then committed myself to taking this secret to the grave. In an attempt to get away from this pain, I would abuse myself with pornography, drugs, sex, and anything else I could find to help me avoid feeling my painful emotions.

Decades later I would come to find out when I turned forty-four that my childhood friend who was sexual towards me was not abused by his parents. Instead he was abused by another child who had a sexually abusive father. The shameful part held by the father was installed into his child and passed along to all of the other kids in the neighborhood. The ripple effect of pain caused a massive tidal wave of drug addiction, sexual compulsion, lies, and manipulation.

It wasn't until I could fully accept that dark shadow part within myself that I would heal and find inner peace. This freedom of my spirit had to be an inside-out game through my body. No matter how hard my overachieving people-pleaser part tried to help me get away from the uncomfortable sensations stored in my body. I would never find relief until I started to accept, love, and learn what was inside of me.

If you've ever had any type of dark night of the soul, you can appreciate what I'm referring to. In my experience divorce, rape, murder, cheating, lying, manipulation, suicide, and certain sicknesses all come from unresolved pain, that in a lot of ways, weren't even our trauma. It was an unhealed part that got passed on a long time ago. Until we take full responsibility for that part and love and accept it with our spirit, we will continue to resist and judge that part that keeps us stuck in our own internal hell.

Think about all the things you don't like or judge about yourself. When and where did you pick up that belief and is it even true?

After spending half of my life unwinding these unhealed wounds, I have learned that life is a constant choice. Depending on where I'm choosing from, this is what creates my current reality and experience. If I choose from scarcity and survival, which is a state of fight, flight, or freeze, then my inner critic will start judging a situation to help me be safe. Unfortunately this keeps me stuck in my pain as my inner critic is a negative belief about myself or others, which generates a negative experience I don't like.

If I choose from a safe and resourceful state, I can tap into my highest self, which is divine intelligence connected to my spirit. This can be as simple as stopping the mental pattern that prevents me from accepting, loving, and learning from my emotions. A lot of times we judge how we feel, which is an inner-critic pattern. This keeps us spiraling downwards and doesn't allow one to feel and heal what is in our bodies.

Through loving and accepting all of our parts and mastering these two choices, we can generate a habit that can empower us to resolve any unhealed wounds from the past. We can then repattern a new belief and take action in the areas we value most.

The beginning of generating any new habit is always uncomfortable. This is what normally stops us from taking more action in the areas that are most harmed.

In the end when I finally got a chance to speak in front of the group of souls at Mark's funeral, I shared from my heart what I believed to be true. I said, "Mark loved everyone here, and I don't believe it was his intention to die."

I also shared, "I was a heroin addict myself and a lot of what Mark chose to do was to get away from his pain."

After I shared my truth I stopped using heroin. Although it would take me another twenty-five years of inner work, love, and acceptance to let go of my shame.

I love you all. I hope this story opens a doorway of possibility so you can start to see that your spirit supersedes all of the pain and trauma of the past. We are all just one thought, one breath, one moment away from healing and accepting the next part of ourselves that was separated a long time ago.

Overtime I overcame gambling, pornography, co-dependence, heroin, cocaine, alcohol, and addiction to sex, scarcity, fear, and worry by accessing the love of God and tapping into my spirit. You have this same access to this choice as well. Together we can collectively heal the planet by focusing on loving ourselves first. Blessings on your journey as we enter into this new time and space of full consciousness here and now.

Eight

Why Captain Morgan Got Fired from My Ship

How to Sail the Seas Sober With Genuine Fun

JILL LAWRENCE

"He doesn't have a mother. I'll be his mother!" I slurred, slumped on the makeshift bed of the pop-up infirmary with a stray cat held hostage in my lap.

Just a few hours before landing my drunk tan ass in the tropical medical ward, I had been one of seventy-five tourists traveling by bus to the luau. The only one who snuck in a bottle of my favorite rum, The Captain, I exited that bus shipwrecked. At nineteen years old I rationalized I had plenty of time to be responsible later. I was here to party after all. And I always keep my promise!

My fuzzy memories of the night include my little sister, Stephanie, finding me outside the bathroom with a Hawaiian lei hanging around my neck and an arm hanging around the neck of a woman much too old to support me.

"Stephanie! Meet Ester! She's the coolest fuckin' grandma I've ever met! I seriously love you, Ester!"

My sister apologized profusely shifting me from Ester's shoulder to hers. I was more toasted than the pig in the pit, and Stephanie had no choice but to take me to the infirmary. The medical staff quickly reported I was drunk and needed to sleep it off. Since I never actually made it inside the bathroom, I had to pee and I'm beyond embarrassed to admit this now, just let loose right there. I'm appalled when I remember watching one of the physicians scrounge around on the floor cleaning it up.

"I did not go to med school for ten years to clean up some drunk girl's piss off the goddamn floor!"

Do they make apology baskets for that? I owe him one!

Accompanied by my horrified sister, Stephanie, and best friend, Lindsey, I tried to get on the bus with the little Hawaiian homeless kitten, but the driver was having none of it. I was not allowed on the bus with or without kitty due to my state of intoxication, and we had to find our own way home. This was pre-ride-share times, and luckily, we bummed a ride from a random Samoan dude. Thankfully, he was a nice guy and we made it back to my dorm room safely. This is just one of oh so many times when I got lucky, and I am forever grateful for my guardian angel (for sure a previous alcoholic) spreading those protective wings over me.

I spent that summer at University of Oahu adding three classes to my transcripts and other similar stories to my "Why I Quit Drinking" list.

It began as a whisper. I'd quickly brush the thought aside assuring myself, *Nah, Jill you're too young for that title. An alcoholic?*

That whisper, although very low and in the background, irritated my mind. Concerned my mind. Yet that mind was often tipsy, drunk, or stoned, allowing the whisper to be washed down along with smart, conscious choices. I justified my concerns with comebacks like, "I never drank throughout high school because I'm an athlete. It wasn't until Christmas break of senior year I started partying. I'm sure everyone forgets chunks of the night. I graduated college with a great GPA. My laundry and home are always clean. I'm cool. Right?"

It's effortless creating excuses for bad habits, isn't it?

We all get wrapped up in excessive destructive actions. Mine was drinking, but this isn't just about drinking. Whether it's shopping, eating, gambling, porning, or mindlessly scrolling social media, these unhealthy habits create an inaccurate reality of your life. We all wear our masks, and the work is learning to show vulnerability and remove the cover-up to find what makes us happy and at peace with ourselves. Genuinely express who you are. Find the comfort in the discomfort. There's nothing more empowering and healing than breaking up with your vice, taking the mask off, while down and dirty looking at the real you. Discard the traumas, excuses, hurts, and low-vibe emotions that encouraged the cover-up in the first place.

We all desire to be seen, heard, and understood. Ironically, the version we display while under the influence is not the true you who needs to be validated in its most vulnerable form. People use alcohol as their shitty sidekick to say or do things they know are unacceptable. Easier said than done, pour the liquor down the drain and garbage dispose that false fire. Courage is speaking from the heart or from a place of truth that takes real strength, not spirits. It takes effort, it takes cajones, to be aware of the thoughts we have flowing through our head every day. We must deal with the realities rising to the surface with a clear head rather than burying them only to be discovered later, four drinks deep. Believe me, that cocktail umbrella will not protect you from the heat.

When people struggle with happiness, confidence, fitting in, or just looking for a mood shift, we are conditioned to turn to alcohol. Feel stuck in life? Take a shot. Boring and blah? Babe, here's a beer. Sad? Have another! Have we ever asked ourselves if the 'happy' in Happy Hour is just that hour and the twenty-three following hours elicit much different emotions? In reality, alcohol and addictions are disempowering and disable drive.

I was under the delusion that I could drink "normal," a.k.a. not black out forgetting portions of the night, emasculating bartenders for pouring weak drinks or mooning tourists on Hollywood Blvd.

I'll only drink until 10 p.m., after that, only water. No shots, just mixed drinks.

Or the infamous tally marks on the hand and when the fifth horizontal line crossed the four pillars, that's it! I'll stop for the night. Instead, I awoke the next morning on my buddy's couch and saw more than ten tally marks littering my hand. My eyes narrow as I reach for my first cup of coffee insinuating, "Don't even ask about the hand graffiti buddy!"

Ugh! There's got to be a way I can control myself when I drink! Every other area of my life is under control. I can overcome this drinking dementia.

Clearly I'm writing about sobriety, so spoiler alert, I couldn't. This was a problem outside of myself that I had to resolve inside of myself. Attaining guidance and wise words from others was a tool that supported my healing and continues to be one of the best tips I pass along. I read voraciously! I learn like my life depends on it. Every mundane task, laundry, dishes, driving...I listen to personal development, self-help, or something motivational to improve my health and overall life. I haven't showered alone in years. Some of the greatest leaders are zest fully clean with me!

Brendon Burchard talks about knowing when it's time to let go because that thing no longer serves you. He calls it, 'The Gambler's Dilemma.' We keep thinking it will get better, but the longer we stay in something that doesn't serve us, it just creates unhappiness and prevents the opportunities for something else that's a better fit. Screw the skinny jeans and skinny margaritas, redefine for yourself what you want, not what others say you should want. As the saying goes, "Don't should all over yourself."

In my early twenties, many of my friends partied the way I did, which normalized the missing memories and midday mimosas. My Grandpa Alvin affirmed to us kids, "You choose your friends, you choose your future."

Are you listening to friends who are unqualified, unhealthy, and maybe even unhappy? Giving up or releasing an addiction benefits your emotional and mental health. As a health and nutrition coach, I'd argue it's just as important for your physical body, brain, and overall well-being.

My initial intention when I stopped partying was to "get my act together." I even shook on it with my brother.

"Done. Starting today, I will not drink, smoke pot, or do any single substance that will alter my state. Jeff, I promise to you for three months I will be clean and sober and get my shit together."

He hugged me not knowing that for the remainder of his life, he'd be hugging a sober sister. That was September 2006. I was twenty-five. This playful gentleman's shake will forever be the most important and life-changing pact I've ever made. In writing this today in 2024, I'm almost eighteen years sober, baby!

In reflection, I never really had one ultimate rock bottom, but rather a passport stamped full of embarrassing and painful stories. I did ruin every single family vacation while drinking. Sorry, Mom! What happened in Vegas did not stay in Vegas! Those bad habits followed me home, and I continued to play roulette by justifying my actions.

When I broke up with my lovers, The Captain and Jack, I developed booze boundaries. With all things, any change happens with how you identify yourself. I no longer identified as someone who drank and couldn't control herself. I now identified as someone who could have a good time and not act a fool. Our words are powerful. Our thoughts guide us and our choices define us.

In losing the addiction, I gained control of my entire life. I rediscovered authentic Jill, and I liked her! By implementing numerous self-care methods, examining why I did or didn't take certain actions, and addressing the real-life emotions that arose, I began healing what the negative behaviors had covered up. At twenty-five, I really invested myself into therapy. Hearing your thoughts, revelations, discoveries, and improvements aloud with the guidance of a professional is priceless! The relief felt from a human holding space for your tears rather than a pint of ice cream is also much healthier.

Recognizing where you need to forgive yourself and others might just be one of the most impactful rituals in healing. Do you feel powerless and want to take your power back? Start with giving back that drink!

Maybe you're in a funk, lost your mojo, and struggling to get that fire under your ass. You ain't gonna light it from drinking a flaming B-52! We are marketed to and under the impression that alcohol will start the party, make us more fun, and take the edge off. Ironically, it often ends the party early with us stumbling out, supported by unimpressed friends. That so-called edge we were looking to 'take off' actually sharpened.

With a background in stand-up comedy, I can confidently declare that humor helps everything! When we get too serious, we lose happiness and the desire to eat well, practice nutritious habits, and feel optimistic. I let bullshit from other people affect me for years! I people pleased, said yes to things I wanted to say hell no to, and held on to old stories. Put them to bed! You have the option to give yourself the happy ending!

Our overall health is so much more than what we eat. It's what we say, don't say, how we move or don't move, who we hang out with, and moving through pain and anger in a quick and healthy way with proper tools and guidance. With encouragement from my cousin, Christine, I joined AA in my twelfth year of sobriety and learned the three principles—recovery, unity, and service—which I rely on today to maintain my physical, mental, and spiritual health.

It's much easier to blame everyone else for our pain and frustrations; however, when you take responsibility for the choices you make and what part you play in all those choices, you step into your power. My whole life I've naturally been a leader. I love helping, supporting, cheerleading, sticking up for, and being the best wingman for everyone—humans and animals alike! I constantly learn, grow, and do, so I can be better for you! Is this an addictive behavior, too? Hell yes, it is! Hi, I'm Jill and I'm a productivity-aholic. It's a delicate dance, and I often overdo it, which can lead to depletion.

I actively work to say no to things and be conscious about where I spend my time. When you declare the priority in life is you, everything can change. I say "can" because you must make the choice and then take action.

Declare: "I'm ready for this positive shift. It's time for me. I'm a priority. I am worth it."

One of the most important tools in reducing addiction is serving others. Giving back gets you out of your own small world. Helping others helps you! I find that volunteering at my local animal shelter resets my soul and decreases the need for unhealthy habits. I may also be addicted to adopting pit bulls.

What is important to you? It can be visiting an elderly home, mentoring children, volunteering in a soup kitchen, or letting someone in during traffic. You're allowed to curse under your breath while waving them in. Progress not perfection.

By re-teaching myself how to have fun, be courageous, silly, and irreverent with nothing fueling those qualities but what's already inside me, and inside of you too, I've positively impacted countless lives.

For the last eighteen years, although not easy, I've lived more open, raw, and vulnerable, which has acted like crazy glue for the most intimate and real connections. Most importantly, to myself. Yeah, yeah, self-love. But yeah, fuck yeah, it all begins with loving yourself so deeply, you desire to derail from destructive behaviors.

As shame researcher Brene Brown preaches, "Vulnerability is the core of shame and fear and our struggle for worthiness, but it appears that it's also the birthplace of joy, of creativity, of belonging, of love."

When you catch yourself reaching for a nonsense cover-up, take a meaningful deep inhale and then a long exhale restoring your nervous system and ask yourself, *What is the most authentic way I can respond to this?*

Now do that, you badass!

A life lived in integrity, while taking full responsibility for all outcomes provides personal empowerment, natural boundaries, and a protective layer where you get to instill your happiness and contentment with life. There will never be an outside source, substance, or addiction that will generate true peace and joy.

I don't believe everyone needs to be or should be sober. But I do wish for everyone to have a true connection to themselves. Attend your own personal AA by implementing awareness and action. As we release addiction, we increase positivity, self-confidence, improve relationships, all while creating that awareness around our choices and habits.

One of the best feelings we can give ourselves is pride in accomplishment.

Being proud is not accomplished because you did the damn thing well; it's that you did the damn thing you were afraid of. You moved forward with courage, and can look at how far you've come and say, *Wow. I'm proud of myself and the person I am today.* Never again kicked off the bus, because bitches, I'm drivin'. Stray animals welcome!

Nine

My Smile Isn't Worthless. It's Priceless.

Overcoming Financial Abuse to Reclaim My Power

MEGAN MUNSELL

I was unable to control the trembling of my jaw. I had been in this same chair at least five times during the past sixteen years for precisely the exact same reason.

I have shitty teeth.

I can't decide if I won the genetic lottery, or if the hard water in the rural Michigan town where I grew up was to blame.

There's something unnerving about the dentist—especially when you're there because you know you can't ignore the dull ache in your mouth, or you get tired of chewing food only on one side.

I tried to focus on the pressure of the electric blood pressure cuff. For a brief second, my focus was on something other than the worst-case scenarios in my mind.

"Your blood pressure is one-forty over ninety-five. When was the last time you saw your primary care doctor?"

"I had an annual exam three weeks ago." Technically it wasn't a lie, but I didn't want to admit that I hadn't seen a primary care doctor since well before the Covid-19 pandemic. I saw my OBGYN annually, only because I wanted to avoid a fate worse than death: getting pregnant.

"Your blood pressure is a tad high."

"I'm just nervous." An understatement of the century. I felt as if I were being chased by a bear, only I had to sit in this clear-plastic coated leather chair.

The assistant disappeared from the room for a moment and came back with a warm blanket.

"They aren't doing surgeries today, so we had some extra blankets in the warmer. It should help you calm your nerves."

The maternal and caring instinct of the dental assistant was a stark contrast to the fear I felt. I knew that my anxiety was unfounded and a little absurd. Throughout the five tooth implant surgeries and seven implants I had at this very clinic, I had experienced nothing but kindness.

Three of the implants were because my former partner would force me to get teeth pulled if I needed anything more than a simple filling.

One time, I needed a root canal. The dentist office told me that my after-insurance cost would be four-hundred and fifty dollars.

"Do you honestly think you're worth four-hundred and fifty dollars?" My partner sneered at me as I was crumpled up into a ball on the floor unable to control the trembling of my jaw. Trying to hold back the tears was futile.

"You're ugly as fuck anyways. No one will even notice the missing teeth."

The next day, I got that tooth pulled, packed the hole full of gauze, and taught an accounting course at the local university where I served as adjunct professor of accounting.

I drove that day and don't worry. I wasn't on pain meds because the one person in the world who was supposed to love me more than anything told me the reason I had to get my tooth pulled was because I didn't "brush my teeth correctly." By sitting in pain, they said I'd remember it and "do better next time."

I think they were their happiest every time they made me die a little more inside.

To be honest, I went to the classroom to relax. My students were primarily working adults and appreciative of two hours of quiet study time with me there to answer questions. One student even left his seat and returned twenty-five minutes later with an ice pack.

I am so thankful I was allowed to keep a job and be around normal people during this period of my life. Small acts of kindness like this left questions in my soul, ones that gnawed at me until I could admit I was being mistreated.

In the book, *The Body Keeps the Score,* Dr. Bessel Van Der Kolk discusses when someone has a traumatic event, it can be so overwhelming to their system that the brain is unable to process the trauma. Because of that, the trauma is always present. It's not part of the past.

At the dentist office, I wasn't sitting in the chair waiting to speak to the kind surgeon about my eight tooth implant. I was crumpled up on the floor, jaw trembling while being told I was worthless.

This is going to be a hell of a lot more expensive than four fifty.

Having traveled back to one of the most traumatic parts of my past, I'm surprised I didn't stand up, remove the little paper napkin from my neck, and leave the clinic—never to return.

When I tell someone new this story, the first thing they typically say is something along the lines of "were you guys broke?" That would be the logical conclusion. After all, what type of person would block the other from getting dental work needed to retain the function of their teeth?

At that point in our lives, spending hundreds of dollars on a root canal would have been to us the financial equivalent of eating at a fast-food restaurant. I had a corporate job, a growing real estate portfolio, adjunct professor of accounting positions at various schools, and an online consulting gig that brought in nearly twenty-thousand dollars per month.

The shame I felt about my situation wasn't just that I had missing teeth or was told I was worthless on a daily basis—it was far more sinister. I was suffering from financial abuse in a way that made me question my very worth around the foundation of my career: money.

Worse yet, I was gaslit into thinking I wasn't experiencing abuse. After all, the cash accounts were in my name and at any time, I could have wiped the accounts out and made my escape. Instead, I followed painstakingly detailed requirements on what I could spend money on and what I had to ask for permission.

Oh, and did I mention I'm a Certified Public Accountant? At the time of my life where I found myself in this situation, I was a money expert in control of the accounting for millions of dollars at a large corporation, but I felt as though I had no agency over my money.

Call it imposter syndrome on steroids. Who wants a money expert who can't even control their own money?

Oh, the lies we tell ourselves.

When I escaped, I knew I could lose everything I had ever worked for during my entire life, including my life savings and all my investments. I didn't care. At least then I could buy a soda at the gas station without being told that I was terrible with money, and that if they weren't there to tell me how to budget my finances, I'd be on the streets.

I consider myself lucky that I got out of that situation. The mere fact I was able to follow through with leaving can be attributed to the belief you have to reach the point in which you would rather die than live the way you live. I reached that point. To truly live, I had to be willing to die. Staying in fear meant staying in a prison of my own making.

The clinking of keys walking down the hallway brought me back to the present day. The oral surgeon walked in, smiling from ear to ear. He looked almost identical to how I remembered him, only with a few more gray hairs and a few more happy wrinkles around his eyes.

"How's my favorite patient!" He reached out to shake my hand. "Let's see what's going on."

"I guess I'm your favorite patient because I have the equivalent of a small car in my mouth," I said. I always joked with him about the cost of dental work.

"No, you're my favorite patient because you actually take care of your teeth, and I have a suspicion your problems are genetic. Hard to tell without a DNA test. But you don't smoke, you don't have a bunch of plaque. We can tell when people don't take care of their mouth."

"Thank you for not judging me." The weight of six elephants lifted from my shoulder. The trembling in my jaw started to lessen.

He stayed focused on studying the X-rays of my mouth and added, "If I were to judge you, then what if you said to yourself that there was no point in oral care? My job isn't to judge you but to keep your mouth healthy."

I chuckled. Of course this makes sense! I say almost the exact same thing to my accounting clients when they come to me for their financial checkup. I never judge anyone based on what they are or aren't doing financially because the mere fact they set up time with me means they are willing to take their finances seriously.

I smiled to myself. The Universe loves irony. We always teach the lesson we most need to learn ourselves.

The implant costs more than four thousand dollars, and my insurance won't cover it. I prepaid for it on my medical credit card and called it a day. I am worth it, and I deserve it.

I have been away from the abuse for nearly a decade, and I've come a long way. For many years I was in survival mode. Every survivor of abuse or dysfunction needs to find tools and structures to retrain their brain how to think and act within normal society.

We have to get really resourceful, and open up our minds to trying new things. It's rarely simple or easy, but I am a firm believer that once you show the Universe you mean business, it will deploy tools you need to succeed. It is up to you to recognize these tools and deploy them in your healing journey.

For me, the first tool to appear was community. No one wants to feel alone, and community provides the healing balm that brings you back to center. When you have a strong community to offer support and understand your trials and tribulations, healing isn't something to hope for—it's a certainty.

The first community to appear for me was a support group for women in controlling relationships hosted by a Memphis area megachurch. Through that group I realized I was not alone. There were C-suite executives of major companies, lawyers, doctors, therapists, pharmacists, chiropractors, veterinarians, and teachers who all experienced similar life situations.

I was not even the only accountant in the group. We all experienced some sort of financial abuse.

It was amazing to see how our lives were all so different, yet our experience was much the same. It was almost like we were all married to the exact same man. Through our discussions we learned about setting appropriate boundaries, how to parent with a high-conflict co-parent, and how to build the self-esteem necessary to avoid having similar patterns in the future.

We also learned the things we experienced were not our fault. We simply loved the wrong person because of programming we received early in our childhood. Loving the wrong person had nothing to do with our intelligence, professional abilities, worthiness as mothers, or any other character flaw.

When I realized making the decision to love the wrong person did not take away from my professional abilities, I felt freedom. In fact, my ability to hold space for people with complex stories makes me a better accountant. I use the patience and self-love I developed during this period of my life each and every day.

As I've moved on from the initial part of my healing journey, I still find community invaluable. I also find that when I set an intention to pursue a specific goal, communities will pop up to support me. It's truly magical.

For example, I have a big goal of becoming a *New York Times* bestselling author and sought after public speaker. I do not find it ironic that after setting that intention with myself and speaking it out loud to someone else, I discovered a community that would assist me with just that.

But community alone isn't enough.

The thing about healing as part of a community that isn't talked about enough is that to be an effective member of any community, you must do hard inner work. The longer you fight this truth, the more miserable you will be during your healing.

Most will find a lot of resistance around this work, and I was no exception. My ego felt threatened when forced to explore my role in the decisions I made that led to my situation. Dissolving that resistance was possible once I discovered Tarot and Astrology.

I know what you're thinking...a CPA who likes tarot and astrology?! *Quelle horreur!* Astrology is a complex science that has been studied by multiple cultures for millennia. Its use was gatekept by the wealthiest of the wealthy until newspaper horoscopes were popularized in the late 1800s.

Tarot is also a practice that is structured and loosely based on commonly accepted rules and archetypes. It's a tool of pattern recognition and creativity. When you consider these two tools in the context of pattern recognition and true science, then you can see how these mystical tools are perfect for someone with an analytical brain who wants to step into their creativity.

For me, it's not at all about predicting the future or relying on a deck of cards or sky math to make important decisions. On the contrary, I use these tools in my spiritual practice to unlock messages from my higher self that have been tucked away by years of trauma and dissociation.

I use them to better understand why I may have been predisposed to acting or feeling a certain way. This information provides power in helping me become the best version of myself. Pausing before making a big decision because of a pending astrological transit does not mean you are giving away your power. It means you are giving yourself space to ensure the decision you made is the right one for you.

Consulting a tarot or oracle deck to think of possibilities that could arise in a personal or business relationship will unlock thoughts, fears, and desires you already have. It does not take away your personal power unless you allow it to.

Your trauma does not define you or your abilities. Experiencing financial abuse, or any other abuse, does not define your abilities professional or otherwise. Healing from this trauma requires both community and inner work that helps you learn how to accept others and, more importantly, yourself. This work will never end, but find the tools that make your soul sing and you'll enjoy every minute of it.

Ten

Rewriting My Story

From Divorce to Empowerment

DEANNA COYLE

H ave you ever had a time in your life that was so challenging you did not know how you would get through it?

I have. For me, it was sixteen years ago.

It was August of 2008. There I was...the mother of two young boys
and newly separated from my husband of ten years.

I was looking around my small, rundown apartment while agoniz-
ing over how to revamp my resume.

After five years out of the workforce as a stay-at-home mom, how
would I regain my footing in the highly competitive financial services
industry? I felt overwhelmed and lost.

It was time to make dinner and I was putting off that task, which
I normally loved doing. I could not open the door of the oven all the
way because it would bump up against the knob of the cabinet underneath the adjacent kitchen sink.

There I stood in a kitchen so cramped it could double as a broom closet, making dinner with an oven that clearly had trust issues with the cabinet next to it. I found myself longing for the days when I could open my oven door without playing a game of Tetris with my kitchen appliances.

It wasn't always like this. Just a few weeks prior, I was living what appeared to be an ideal life in a beautiful home in a friendly neighborhood where the majority of the women were stay-at-home moms.

I had left my career as a securities analyst on Wall Street to become a stay-at-home mom focusing on our family while my husband focused on his career. My husband increased his salary substantially, and we built considerable equity in our home and saved money for our retirement and our childrens' education. Our kids went to private school, and I loved to cook and throw dinner parties for our friends and neighbors.

I enjoyed the feeling of community and family around which we built our life. My typical day consisted of bringing my kids to preschool; running errands; going to yoga classes; picking my kids up from school; hosting play dates; making dinner; and getting the kids ready for bed.

Then everything came crashing down when my husband and I separated and decided to divorce.

THE BREAKING POINT

In June of 2008, my husband and I were on vacation in Maine with the boys. He and I were arguing about who was going to go into the grocery store to buy sandwiches for the boys.

I said, "I'll go in and get them, I know just where they are."

"No, I'll go in!" he insisted.

After a couple of minutes of going back and forth, my husband went into the store to buy the sandwiches. I was fuming in the front seat and wondering why we bickered over such minor things. All of a sudden, I heard a small voice coming from the back seat.

"Mommy," my six-year-old son, Sean, said. "Why do you and Daddy fight all the time?"

I turned around to comfort him and realized he and our other son (four-year-old Ryan) looked upset. I was so focused on the argument with my husband that I had forgotten Sean and Ryan were within earshot.

The truth is, this argument was just the tip of the iceberg. The small disagreements had become more frequent, and each one seemed to escalate more quickly than the last. We were constantly on edge, tiptoeing around each other, and the smallest thing could set off another round of bickering. It wasn't just about who would go into the grocery store or what to have for dinner; it was about everything. There was tension over finances, parenting decisions, and household responsibilities.

Our home, which once felt like a sanctuary, now felt like a battleground. The boys, who had once been blissfully unaware of any discord between their parents, were beginning to sense the growing tension. I could see the confusion and sadness in their eyes, and it broke my heart.

As the weeks went by, the arguments became more intense. We began to retreat into our own corners, emotionally distancing ourselves from each other. I was constantly on edge, always waiting for the next argument to erupt. We both said things we didn't mean, things that left wounds that couldn't be easily healed. It was as if we were trapped in a cycle of negativity, and neither of us knew how to break free.

The final straw came one evening when the boys were playing in the living room, and my husband and I started arguing about something so insignificant that I can't even remember what it was. But what I do remember is the way it escalated so quickly, with voices raised and tempers flaring. Sean and Ryan were sitting quietly on the couch, their toys forgotten, watching us with wide, scared eyes.

At that moment, I looked at their faces and realized the impact our constant fighting was having on them. They were no longer the happy, carefree children they had been. They were tense, anxious, and unsure of what might happen next. I could see the fear in their eyes, the fear that their world was falling apart, just like mine had when I was their age.

It hit me like a ton of bricks: I was repeating the cycle. The very thing I had feared most—subjecting my children to the same pain and confusion I had felt during my own parents' divorce—was happening right before my eyes.

That night, after the boys had gone to bed, I sat alone in the living room, tears streaming down my face. I knew I couldn't keep doing this to them—or to myself. It was time to make a change, no matter how difficult it would be. I couldn't control what my husband did or said, but I could control my own actions. I could choose to break the cycle.

Two months later, I moved out of our beautiful home and neighborhood into a small apartment to stop subjecting Sean and Ryan to the ever-increasing arguments. It was one of the hardest decisions I had ever made, but I felt it was my only choice at the time.

A MOMENT OF REFLECTION

As I stood in my small kitchen, I wondered, "How did I end up here?"

This was not the life I had envisioned and worked so long and hard to attain. I had worked for years in the grueling financial services industry, received my masters of business administration (MBA) from a top business school, and achieved the hard-to-obtain Chartered Financial Analyst designation. I had finally attained what I thought was my dream career as a securities analyst on Wall Street making money I never imagined earning.

As I looked around my small apartment, a stream of questions went through my mind.

"How was I ever going to get through this?"

"Would I ever rebuild my career to support myself and my children?"

"Would I ever rebuild my social life?"

"How would I be a great role model for my boys and raise them to be the amazing men I knew they were capable of being?"

"How would I stop the pattern of divorce and turmoil, which started with my grandparents, then my parents, and finally me, from extending to my boys?"

My divorce took three years and it was long, arduous, and emotionally and financially draining. After my divorce finalized, I did a lot of self-evaluation and personal and professional development work. I realized something that happened when I was young shaped how I was living my life and held me back from true happiness.

UNCOVERING THE PAST TO HEAL THE PRESENT

When I was five years old, my parents divorced and my mom moved out of state. I lived with my dad and I remember when my mom would come to visit–it wasn't often. I would ask her to stay with us and did not understand why she had to leave.

I remember thinking, *If only I were a better daughter, then my parents would not be apart and we could all live together again.*

Of course, my parents' divorce was about them and not about me. However, I did not know that at the time. I had gone through life thinking that I was not good enough and that people leave. As an adult, I would take actions to make that a self-fulfilling prophecy.

For example, I would start a relationship and tell the person that I was not good at relationships. Then I would proceed to take actions that would cause the relationship to end. I did not trust myself or my partner.

The relationship would end and I would say, "See, I was right. I'm not good enough and I'm not good at relationships."

Because I lived my life that way, my relationships suffered. My self-limiting beliefs influenced my decisions and behaviors throughout my life, without me even realizing it.

I began to face my fears and work on transforming myself and my life. Through reflection, therapy, and positive self-talk, I was able to recognize my limiting beliefs and transform them over time.

A defining moment for me occurred about four years after my divorce. I had been dating my boyfriend for about two years, and we were going out to dinner. We parked the car and walked to the front door while holding hands.

As we looked inside the restaurant, my boyfriend said, "Oh bummer. It is crowded. I don't think we'll get seats at the bar. We'll have to sit at a table."

I removed my hand from his and said, "Oh how awful! You may even have to make conversation with me!"

As soon as I did that, I saw a look of confusion and sorrow cross his face. I immediately realized that my self-limiting beliefs of not feeling good enough caused me to think he didn't want to be close to me. In reality, at that restaurant, it was often hard to get prompt service unless you were sitting at the bar.

I took back his hand and said, "I'm so sorry. I know you just want to sit at the bar so we will get quicker service."

He smiled and said, "Yes."

We went on to have a wonderful night.

In the past, I would have stayed upset with him for hours (maybe even days). I would have let that small comment fester and grow into something much larger, convincing myself that it was a sign of deeper issues. Instead, I chose to address it head-on, acknowledging my insecurities and giving my partner the benefit of the doubt.

My ability to self-reflect and work on my self-limiting beliefs has changed my life. I am now happier and more empowered than ever.

FROM CHALLENGES TO TRIUMPHS

In 2013, I began building a business—Vesta: A New Vision for Divorce—that focuses on transforming the divorce process so others can benefit from what I learned. In the past eleven years, we have helped over ten thousand people.

Through my struggles and triumphs, I discovered that we can all turn our challenges into opportunities for crafting a life we love. I invite you to take whatever adversity you have faced in the past or are currently facing and use it as a catalyst for positive transformation. By recognizing and overcoming self-limiting beliefs, you can unlock your true potential and create a fulfilling and joyful life. Embrace your journey, and remember that every challenge is an opportunity for growth and transformation.

Have you ever tried to fit a square peg into a round hole? That was me in my cramped kitchen attempting to make a gourmet meal with an oven that had a personal vendetta against the cabinet next to it. Isn't that life sometimes? We try to fit into roles or situations that just don't work, and we end up feeling stuck and frustrated.

Here's the thing—those challenges, those moments when we feel like we're failing, are the very experiences that shape us. They push us to grow, adapt, and discover strengths we never knew we had. My journey taught me that resilience isn't about never falling; it's about getting up every time we do.

If you're facing a tough time, remember you are stronger than you think. Sometimes, it takes the most challenging situations to reveal your true strength. Don't be afraid to face your fears, challenge your self-limiting beliefs, and embrace the journey. On the other side of that struggle is a life you never imagined possible—one filled with joy, fulfillment, and endless possibilities.

Life has a funny way of throwing curve-balls when we least expect them. But those curve-balls can turn into home runs if we learn to swing the bat with confidence. Take my story as proof that even when you're stuck playing Tetris with your kitchen appliances, you can still cook up a life full of success and happiness.

If you find yourself in a cramped kitchen of life, keep in mind that it's just a chapter, not the whole story. Laugh at the absurdities, learn from the challenges, and keep pushing forward.

You have the power to rewrite your story. Your best days are ahead of the challenges!

Eleven

Answering the Call

Love Through the Theta State

GWEN ALYSSA GAYDOS

The Covid-19 pandemic lock-down had only been in place for one month, and here I was again. All I could feel was the heaviness of my heart, the tears streaming down my face, and my body unable to move from the couch.

After an hour or so of my new yet familiar daily routine, oxygen started flowing to my brain again, and the thoughts began to race.

I met a handsome, charismatic, creative guy who didn't live with his mom or four roommates. He pursued me, courted me properly, we had loads of fun, and then after a few months when we started to get closer, he started pulling away, and wham, it was over, just like that.

"I don't know what it is, but it doesn't feel right anymore. I think we need to break up." He told me in a casual tone over our morning coffee.

He gave me no other explanation.

I don't get it. Things seemed like they were going well. What happened? I went over it and over it in my mind trying to figure out what went wrong.

After a couple hours of this, the thoughts continued to gain momentum. Part two of the internal inquisition began.

How did I get here? All I've wanted for the past ten years is a healthy relationship, and I'm alone again. What did I do wrong? I don't understand it. I've done all the work! Therapists, coaches, transformational programs. They always leave. There must be something wrong with me. I guess I'm destined to die alone with ten cats.

My heart sank even deeper. This pattern went on for weeks.

Here I found myself again at what felt like the lowest point on the roller-coaster of despair with my two cats. I felt trapped and tired in my four-hundred-square-foot apartment in Venice, California. I had just experienced another breakup in a string of half-committed, narcissistic, addicted, avoidant, or otherwise mentally imbalanced men.

Was it L.A.? Was it me?

The list was long. There was the toxic party guy who kept sucking me back in, the narcissist drug addict, the avoidant man-child, and the latest, a professional escape artist. These were all short-term runaways, not counting the many blips before, and the four failed long-term relationships, including a failed marriage, confirming my assumption and belief: *There must be something wrong with me. They all leave. It never works out for me in love.*

Over the years I had seen countless therapists, taken every transformational program known to man, hired life coaches, love coaches, and vented to all of my friends, but somehow I still wasn't able to do this love thing. I felt so much shame, so much like a fraud.

Here I am, "Miss healthy." I'm smart, attractive, and I can't even meet and keep a man around for longer than three months! Every time I thought it would be different. But it never was.

To add insult to injury, my work in the world of showbiz had come to a halt, and I was barely working. *What would I do for work? How would I support myself?*

I had been a professional model and actor for many years, along with a holistic health coach. My coaching business also wasn't working for me. The pattern was like this: When I was in a relationship and happy, my work would thrive. When I had a breakup, it felt so terrible, I couldn't bring myself to work. I would fall into a deep depression, I would isolate, and nothing would get done. I felt like I was the passenger on an extreme-thrill roller coaster in the dark, never knowing which way I'd go next. How low I'd go and what was coming next was always a mystery. It was up and down and out of my control. This was my life.

Why can't I get it together? There must be something wrong with me.

THE VOICE

After months of torturing myself with circling thoughts of lies, sleepless nights, friends badgering me, heaps of ice cream, and binge watching every single season of *The Office* for the third time, something inside of me said, *Hi, Gwen. It's time. Pull yourself up. You can't continue this pattern. It's exhausting and destructive to your entire life—body, mind, and spirit. You **have to** figure this out.*

I heard it and knew it was true, and that it was right. It was time. I knew there had to be something I was missing, but what?

When in this place of familiar turmoil, I began where I felt at home. I practiced yoga, took walks on the beach, and journaled every morning, which had saved me in times like these before. One foot in front of the other, no pun intended.

On my walks, I began receiving intuitive messages, one of which was to start listening to Abraham Hicks, one of my all time favorite coaching gurus, and the queen of the law of attraction. My walks helped me get into the moment, be one with nature, and at least see other humans, so I could feel like one again. It helped my emotions flow through me naturally. Yes they hurt, but thank God they were moving. I later learned that walking helps us to process emotions through bilateral stimulation.

As I was listening to Abraham one morning, I stumbled across a Dr. Joe Dispenza video online. I had read some of his work years before but had forgotten about him until this moment. Then it hit me, *This is it! Subconscious reprogramming. I need to rewire my brain!*

From this moment I knew, without a shadow of a doubt, this is what I needed to do. I don't know how I knew, but I just **knew**. This was one of my ways of connecting with my highest self, my intuition. I would just get these "hits" and suddenly **know**.

I had heard of eye movement desensitization and reprocessing (EMDR), and I had studied Bruce Lipton's work on epigenetics, how we can shape the expression of our genes, both of which led me to dive right in. That day I signed up for Dr. Joe's online course, so I could learn to reprogram my brain. I was ripe with enthusiasm.

One of the main practices in Dr. Joe's program was to meditate daily. For a **long** time.

Following Dr. Joe's advice, I began meditating forty-five minutes a day, increasing to an hour per day. This was no joke. I had plenty of experience as a meditator and even taught meditation, and this doubled my normal practice of twenty minutes per day. However, I was dedicated to my personal transformation and sat my butt down every single morning to "feel the space beyond the space" with Dr. Joe. This changed everything.

At first, I was fidgety, and my chattery mind was the boss. Every day it got a little easier. I started feeling lighter, happier, clearer. I began journaling. I learned to smile again.

It's going to be OK.

I started to receive messages.

Become a sound healer.

I started seeing visions.

Me on a beach with these beautiful singing bowls, happy. What was this?

The first sound bath I attended was in 2011, and I couldn't find one again until 2018 when I moved to Los Angeles. It was an emotional experience that left an impression on me. I loved sound healing and had three crystal singing bowls that I played here and there. I wanted to learn, but I had no idea who to hire to teach me, and over these past few months I had given in to fear, panicked, and pivoted.

In search of a new career path, I decided to become a real estate agent. So when I heard this voice, I was like, "Shhhhhh!"

I did the exact thing I would tell my coaching clients not to do. Silence the inner voice.

But I kept meditating, and the messages only became louder. It was super annoying.

Become a sound healer. Become a sound healer!

Now what do I do?

This went on for weeks, months, actually, to be exact, nine months. One morning, I was meditating and the voice was literally yelling at me.

Become a sound healer. Become a sound healer! **Become a sound healer!**

Then I saw the vision again.

Me on the beach with the crystal singing bowls.

The images were so vivid and life-like. I finally caved. I had no other choice. I needed the voice to stop!

I opened my eyes mid-meditation, opened my laptop, and no kidding, the first email in my inbox was from my friend, Susy, who I met at the meditation studio in West Hollywood where I worked as a meditation teacher. She was a successful sound healer and was hosting her first healer mentorship course.

This was it. I knew it. The next step. The Universe is showing me the way and lighting up my path. The email read, "Last day to sign up for a call to apply!" And I did.

I continued to meditate daily with Dr. Joe at least forty-five minutes daily as a committed student. I would journal after most times, and I continued to feel better and better. I was trusting more and fearing less, connecting with my heart more and listening to my intuition. I was healing the pain and letting whatever came up, come up. I lived in the moment more. Since this was all going on during Covid, I enjoyed nature and more solidarity than ever. It was a new way of being for me. After years of living in big cities like New York, Miami, and Los Angeles, I kind of liked it. I didn't know what was next, but I knew I was on the right path.

Little did I know what I would embark on over the next couple of years would lead me to the life and love of my dreams.

THE MISSING LINK

Somehow on a deep level, I knew this was the way through. Subconscious reprogramming. Rewiring the brain. Changing the program that was running me. I was stuck in old patterns I didn't even know were running and ruining my life. Once the floodgates opened, it was game on.

The most significant change I made was to listen. Listen to my intuition. Your intuition is never wrong...ever. How did I do that? I was open to it and determined to figure out what the missing link was to this puzzle. When I heard the words, *You have to figure this out*. I knew it was time. That message and those feelings were my intuition and my deep knowing that it was right, and I could do this.

Glennon Doyle says, "You can do hard things." And I can.

You can too.

From October 2020 to July 2024 my life completely changed. With what started as just a seed of knowingness, came excitement, and then sheer determination to make my life better. To make my dreams come true by changing myself from within, whatever it took.

It started simply with getting outside and walking, then yoga, meditation, and journaling. Next, I amplified the action. I listened to my intuition and hired a healers' business coach with whom I worked with for six months. During this time, I also hired a therapist who specialized in exactly what I needed and combined EMDR with our sessions, which is a subconscious reprogramming tool that I found powerful. I worked with her for nine months, and about three months in, I met an amazing man, with whom I am still in a healthy, happy relationship, two years and counting as of 2024. Some days I still have to pinch myself.

This led me into a sound healer's training, a three-month program, which led me to become a sound healer. I have become so passionate about sound knowing now—it can help us connect to our subconscious minds through brainwave entrainment. This was the cherry on top for me.

My instincts guided me to learn sound healing but I didn't know why. It is such a marvelous synchronicity that sound itself can help us connect to our subconscious minds! It also helps people go deeper into the meditative state and healing brainwave states where we can potentially connect with our subconscious, faster than meditation alone. I have personally experienced this.

Since many people think meditation is hard, or they can't do it, or they can't sit still, or (insert reason or excuse here), it's so incredible to have this offer to share! My eyes well up knowing this may change someone's life on such a deep level.

Not to mention, sound is a beautiful, ancient healing art. For me, expressing myself this way by performing and healing, it is the perfect thing for me to do in this world. These are my gifts to share, and I am thriving and happy doing it.

Since 2021, I have led hundreds of sound baths, privately, corporately, in studios, online, and on the beach just like in my vision! I've spoken in front of many groups about healing frequencies and have now become a sound healer teacher and mentor.

I can't even imagine what would have happened if I didn't listen to that little voice.

If you're curious, I encourage you to experience a sound bath in person or online, and let your mind and body be still. Listen to the sound of the bowls and relax. Remember, you are in charge of your body. You can be still. You will very likely have thoughts at first, and that is normal. Simply direct your attention to a point of focus when noticing thoughts. Many use the breath or the sound of the instruments, or mantra.

Consider making this a daily practice, and watch the magic happen. Journal afterward to jot down insights and messages, and above all, trust your intuition. Follow it. You have all of the answers inside of you, and the Universe wants to co-create the life of your dreams with you!

Sometimes you can't see the light at the end of the tunnel, but I promise, it is there. Keep going. You are exactly where you are supposed to be right now. Trust. Put one foot in front of the other. You can do hard things. **I know it.**

Twelve

Reclaiming Power From Not Being Enough

A Journey from Fear and Self-Doubt to Self-Empowerment

KEENA ALEXANDER

I n the intricate tapestry of my life, a subtle but persistent thread wove itself through every experience, coloring my interactions, shaping my decisions, and stifling my potential. This thread was the nagging, ever-present fear of not being enough. Perhaps it entered my psyche at an unknown but tender age, such as the first time my dear grandmother reminded me that girls were to be seen and not heard. This woman, who loved me so dearly, unconsciously shared with me the trauma she had been forced to navigate. The echoes of this sentiment followed me into my childhood, and one day, my third-grade teacher drove the point home with a devastating comment.

I was a bright-eyed little girl, eager to learn and always quick with the correct answer. My enthusiasm for school was genuine; I loved the feeling of solving problems and grasping new concepts. When my teacher asked me to stay behind after class one afternoon, I thought she wanted to commend my performance. Instead, her words left me stunned.

"I hate having you in my class," she said, her voice devoid of any warmth. "Your good grades are ruining my curve, and I have to work harder because of you."

As I stood there, her words hit me like a physical blow. I didn't understand. How could my good grades be a problem? The room felt suddenly too large and too small all at once. My heart pounded in my chest, and my eyes welled up with tears that I fought to hold back. Her gaze was unyielding, and I realized she wasn't joking. This verbal assault on my nine-year-old spirit was really happening.

From that moment, the fear planted deep within me grew to embody the fruit of distrust and the self-image of not being enough. It was a fear that said no one wanted me; my presence burdened others. The shock of that encounter stayed with me, shaping my interactions and decisions for years to come. This fear extended beyond the classroom, infiltrating my roles as a wife, mother, daughter, and friend. I became invisible to myself. I couldn't make meaningful connections with others, live a purposeful life, or envision a successful future.

Growing up, I was subjected to messages that reinforced my sense of otherness and planted seeds of self-doubt. I vividly remember an elementary school physical education teacher who told me and the other Black girls in my class that most of us would end up as teenage mothers simply because we were from the inner city. The harshness of his words, delivered with an air of certainty, left a mark on me. These experiences were early indicators of how society would view me—not just as a child, but as a Black girl destined for failure.

As I grew older, I became increasingly aware of my double minority status—being both Black and a woman. This intersectionality often pushed me to the margins of societal narratives, a reality that became even more pronounced when I began my career in the Department of Defense. There were numerous challenges I faced: implicit biases, microaggressions, and systemic barriers that constantly questioned my competence and value. In this environment, where unspoken rules and coded language dictated the norms, my fear of not being enough was reinforced daily.

Even the seemingly positive comments from coworkers—remarks about how articulate I was or praise for how well I handled myself—carried an underlying assumption. These compliments suggested that I was an exception to a negative stereotype, a belief that further isolated me and reminded me of the pervasive biases I was up against.

I experienced a visceral response rooted in my subconscious and triggered by the daily realities of my existence. Each slight, each dismissal, each opportunity overlooked or denied chipped away at my sense of self-worth. The fear became a self-fulfilling prophecy, perpetuating a cycle where the desire to be seen and acknowledged only amplified my invisibility and self-doubt.

BEGINNING THE JOURNEY OF HEALING

Fear, particularly the fear of not being enough, is a fundamental barrier to forming deep, authentic connections with others. This self-perpetuating trauma prevented me from truly knowing myself, which, in turn, impeded my ability to connect with those around me. It was a primal response that resided in the lower levels of my consciousness, preventing me from accessing the higher planes of belief and self-empowerment.

In my personal life, this fear manifested in various ways—hesitation to open up, reluctance to trust others, and constant second-guessing of my worth in relationships. It was an insidious force that not only hindered my personal growth but also affected my interactions with friends and family. Because I was invisible to myself, I couldn't form deep connections with others or live aligned with my true purpose. Without a clear vision for myself, I found it challenging to foster genuine relationships. The fear permeated every aspect of my life, from my role as a mother to my interactions with friends and family, casting a shadow over my aspirations and achievements.

The journey to healing began with a simple yet profound realization—recognizing fear for what it was. Fear is not of God; it does not exist on a higher plane of consciousness. It is a construct of the mind, a response to threats—perceived or actual—that creates a decision point: Will I hide, or will I fight? This understanding was a pivotal moment in my journey, marking the beginning of my transformation from a state of fear to one of empowerment. It also underscored the importance of self-reflection and self-forgiveness, two crucial elements in the journey towards self-empowerment.

A life coach friend once asked me a simple and pivotal question, "Keena, who do you want people to know you as?" This question was a turning point in my journey. It made me realize that I was living in fear, hiding from the world and myself. I knew my thoughts, my fears, my desires. But I couldn't articulate what was uniquely me. I realized I hadn't just hidden myself from the world, but I had been hiding from myself, and I would need to find myself in order to present myself.

The first step was to confront the fear, acknowledge its presence, and understand its origins. This transformation required a deep dive into my past, exploring the experiences and societal narratives that had shaped my fear. It was a painful process, bringing to light memories of rejection, marginalization, and self-doubt. However, it was also a liberating one, allowing me to see the fear not as an intrinsic part of my identity but as an external force that I had the power to overcome.

I began to peel back the layers of my fear. The images of ancestors and community elders as large trees blocking my view began to fade into a realization of the shade they provided me and the opportunity to become something other than the destruction and trauma that molded them. Still, I had carried this trauma and needed to let go to find myself.

As Paulo Coelho put it, "Maybe the journey isn't about becoming anything. Maybe it's about unbecoming everything that isn't really you so that you can be who you were meant to be in the first place."

THE PATH TO EMPOWERMENT

Healing from the fear of not being enough was not an overnight transformation; it was a gradual process of inner work and self-discovery. It required a commitment to acknowledging the desire to change, a willingness to face my vulnerabilities, and a determination to reclaim my power.

The journey began with self-reflection, taking an honest look at my life, and acknowledging the areas where fear had held me back. Reflection was coupled with a practice of self-forgiveness, releasing the guilt and shame associated with past failures and mistakes. Forgiveness was crucial in breaking the cycle of self-doubt and opening the door to healing and growth.

Central to my healing was the affirmation of my inherent worth. I challenged the negative self-talk and replaced it with positive affirmations. I learned to celebrate my achievements, no matter how small, and to view setbacks not as reflections of my inadequacy but as opportunities for growth and learning.

Overcoming the fear of not being enough requires building resilience—the ability to bounce back from adversity and persist in the face of challenges. This was achieved through a combination of mindfulness practices, physical self-care, and a supportive network of mentors and peers who provided encouragement and perspective.

At the heart of my transformation was the shift from fear to belief—belief in my abilities, in my worth, and in my right to be seen and heard. This belief was not just a mental construct but a lived experience manifested through my thoughts, words, actions, and habits. It became the foundation of my relationships, enabling me to connect with confidence and authenticity.

The same young girl devastated by her third-grade teacher grew up to be a woman who found herself going through a tough divorce. In the thick of it, I barely functioned. I would take my children to school and drive myself to work, go through the motions at work, then pick up the children and attempt to muster the strength to mother. I was distraught, alone, and felt like a failure. It felt as if I was giving the world what it had expected of me all along.

A dear friend reached out, knowing my journey and my pain. She asked me if I had prayed for God to take away the fear that kept me in pain. This was a novel idea. I believed that the Lord loved me but also that this pain was my plight. My cross to bear. This thought—that I was supposed to bear these crosses—kept me from greatness in other areas of my life and relationships. I had never thought to ask for my pain to be removed. I'd prayed for endurance and grace but not for the pain to cease. That night, my friend prayed with me, and the following day, I awoke equally unexcited to do life. I dropped my kids off at school and planned to drive to work, only to find myself heading toward my home. I couldn't do it anymore. I didn't know how I would go on, but I knew that day I couldn't do much more.

I wandered to my bathroom and turned on the shower. I needed the calming sound of the water running. As I stood there in the water, I found myself embraced in a feeling I'd never felt before. I was afraid and confused. I thought, *Oh great, this is the point where I tip over the edge. I've finally lost myself. I've lost my will.*

Just as quickly as those thoughts entered my head, an indescribable calmness filled my heart. I wasn't having a breakdown. I was at peace. A peace I'd probably never felt before in my life. I heartily laughed as I wrapped my arms around myself, realizing my prayer had been answered. I didn't know much, but I knew I wanted more of this feeling.

Shortly after the shower, my soon-to-be ex-husband called me for the first and last time since we'd begun the divorce. He apologized for his indiscretion and shared the pain he was experiencing. In my newfound peace, I listened, prayed for him, thanked him for his call, and dismissed myself from the conversation. Now free of the fear of not being enough that had been paralyzing me, I was convinced of the need to uncover my identity and reclaim my power.

That profound moment marked the beginning of my reclamation of power. I learned that to heal, I needed to face my fears, confront my pain, not carry it, and allow myself to feel.

I hope to inspire others who grapple with their fears and insecurities, particularly those who, like me, exist at the intersections of multiple marginalizations. Healing is not just a personal journey; it is a collective one—a journey that transforms our wounds into wisdom and our struggles into sources of strength. It is through this process of healing we can reclaim our power, embrace our inherent worth, and lead with courage and conviction.

Thirteen

Letting Light into the Mother Wound

Transforming Deep Pain Into Empowerment and Joy

LAURA LEE PAHA

I stared at the staircase in front of me, then lowered my gaze back down to my tiny, bright-white shoes contrasting against the teal carpet. Crossing from the kindergarten wing to where the "big kids" went to school could be intimidating for a timid five-year-old, but one of the perks of being a teacher's kid was that other teacher's kids were always looking out for me.

The fourth grader gently squeezed my hand, reassuring me, "You're going to be fine!" as she walked me up the stairs.

As we reached the top, I felt safe and grateful to have a buddy in this big, new world of elementary school. She guided me into the bathroom and she kept the friendly conversation going, "My mom told me you're adopted! That is so cool!"

Every sense of calm and comfort evaporated from my body. My face went cold, my chest tightened, and a heavy pit formed in the bottom of my little stomach.

"Yeah..." I responded, my voice trailing off as I forced a smile, let go of her hand, and walked into a stall.

As I sat in the stall, my mind reeled as I tried to comprehend what just happened. I had this sudden epiphany that *none* of my new friends I'd met in my first week of school had mentioned being adopted. Ashley, my new fourth-grade buddy who was looking out for me, brought up adoption as if it was something rare and different. I walked out of the bathroom with a stigma: I was adopted, and I was *different*. In that moment, adoption became my deepest, darkest secret that I had to protect at all costs if I ever wanted to belong in the world.

My deep, dark secret was the one caveat to an otherwise picture-perfect childhood. I grew up to become a mother wound healing expert, but anyone who knew my mom, my parents, or anything about my childhood might wonder *what* mother wounds?! They wouldn't be wrong for wondering.

My childhood was everything it appeared to be. My parents were incredible: loving, warm, devoted to me and to each other, and they did everything they could to give me all of the love and experiences a child could dream. They always gave me permission to be who I wanted to be. They were even open with me about being adopted. I can't remember *not* knowing. It just wasn't something we talked about often, and to be honest, just knowing I was adopted and they were now my loving parents was all I needed to know. It wasn't until that moment in the bathroom in kindergarten that I felt shame around it. That I realized how **different** it made me. To ease the tension in my chest and calm my rapid-fire mind, I tucked it away in a dark corner of myself where I'd rarely think about it again.

I walked out of the bathroom stall and returned to my picture-perfect life. From a young age, I valued and appreciated everything my parents invested in me. I certainly didn't take it for granted. I wanted to make them proud and give them a return on their investment. Of course they had high expectations for me, but nothing compared to the pressure of the expectations I held for myself. Getting a B on a test or not finishing first in soccer sprints had consequences. My mom, the eternal cheerleader, would reassure me of how smart and capable I was, of how she loved me no matter what, and how she knew I'd get it next time. My dad might have some questions about why I fell short of my goals, but it was nothing compared to the self-imposed interrogations I put myself through. Being a perfectionist was like a toxic relationship. It felt awful, but it was also addictive. It was unhealthy, but at times it was also rewarding. The heavy pressure I put on myself molded me into a high-achieving student and athlete. It got me an academic scholarship to college and even acceptance into law school.

Before I started high school, I knew I wanted to be a lawyer. When I graduated with honors, passed the Bar Exam, and landed my first job, I was dumbfounded as to why I felt empty inside. As a perfectionist, emotions got in the way of my goals. Feeling was a waste of time, and I took pride in pushing aside my feelings and staying focused on what mattered. But I was so lost and depressed, I couldn't ignore it. So, I resorted to something I thought was reserved for the weak and mentally ill, therapy.

At my first appointment, my therapist had me create a timeline of my life. As she asked the first question, I instantly regretted my decision, "Do you think your adoption is related to how you're feeling now?"

I resisted rolling my eyes into the back of my skull. *What would that have to do with anything?* All I gave her was a short "No."

Surprisingly, I didn't quit therapy after that, and I benefited from it. I realized helping people was my life purpose but not as an attorney. I found a career in which I could help people through my first love (sports) and use my business savvy as well. My parents helped me load a U-Haul, and I left home and my short-lived legal career to move to Nashville to help open a fitness franchise.

My short stint in therapy also changed my life under the surface in unexpected ways. For the first time, I was willing to be curious about my adoption. I was able to get in touch with a woman who'd been a part of the process, and learned that after my birth mother gave me away, she changed her mind and wanted to see me again. When I was a month old, we met again at a McDonald's. She held me, decided she made the right choice, and gave me back. There was freedom in the truth, and I went to Nashville feeling somewhat free from the pressure of perfectionism, free from the shame of my origin story, and more open to who I was becoming.

After living in Nashville a few years, it felt like my life was all coming together. And just as fast as it came together, it completely fell apart. I was home for Christmas, and the night before I was going back to Nashville, my parents sat me down in such a serious way, I knew something was wrong.

"I had a doctor's visit, and they found a lump in my breast," my mom said softly. "It's cancerous. They're going to perform a mastectomy, then I'll go through chemo and radiation."

The news hit me hard. My mom was my person, and I thought we had decades of life left to enjoy together. *This can't be happening. But women survive breast cancer all the time. It's going to be fine.* I vacillated between hope and despair in my mind, not knowing what to say or how to feel. I returned to Nashville feeling worried, scared, and unsure what to do with all of the big feelings that surfaced inside of me.

I didn't know how I would navigate my mom's diagnosis alone, and suddenly, it seemed like I wouldn't have to. I had been on countless first dates since I relocated, but I never felt that "spark" you were supposed to feel with any of the men. One day at a CrossFit competition, all of that changed.

FACING THE DEPTH OF MY PAIN AND FINDING MY INNER POWER

"Love the shirt," the voice from behind me caught me off guard. I turned around and was face to face with a girl whose magnetism pulled me in hard. We exchanged names and pleasantries, and I went on my way.

Days passed after that competition, and I was still thinking about her. *What is going on?* I was so confused by how I felt. I'd never been attracted to women before, but I couldn't come up with any other explanation for how I felt about Sienna after **one** encounter. I was faced with a new "something that makes me different," but the feelings were so strong, I had no sense of fear or shame about pursuing her or the aftermath of what it might be like to come out. I felt so **clear**.

Within a couple months of meeting, Sienna and I were dating, and it almost felt too good to be true. It seemed as if she'd fallen as hard for me as I fell for her. We spent every waking moment together, and even though it all happened so fast, I never gave it a second thought.

After a few months, just as I was dreaming of a future with her, Sienna flipped a switch. Suddenly the girl who couldn't get enough of me seemed repulsed by me. She was cold. She responded to me with eye-rolls and insults, or simply gave me the silent treatment. A pervasive fear, more powerful than what I felt sitting in that bathroom stall as a kid, invaded every cell of my body. I had this amazing love, the kind we dream of, and it was vanishing without explanation.

One afternoon, Sienna asked me to go to lunch. She explained that she thought she was in love with me, but she was just confused. She didn't feel "the spark" with me, and I wasn't exciting enough for her. She needed more. She asked me to give her space. I was respectful and gave her what she asked for. I was devastated. This had to be what losing everything felt like—my mom and the one thing I'd longed for: true love. But if it was meant to be, it would find a way.

Within a few weeks, Sienna wanted me back. For the next year, the cycle repeated of her falling for me, then wanting nothing to do with me, dismissing me without hesitation. Every time we reconciled she was colder, harsher, and found new ways to torture me emotionally. Eventually she met a guy and said she was willing to date both of us. That's when I knew I had to get out. My mom's cancer was getting worse, my heart was shattered, and my emotions felt too big to manage.

I tried therapy again. We talked about why I was attached to Sienna, why it was hard to leave, and how it probably all connected back to my adoption. Having the awareness was helpful, but it didn't help me get out of the situation. Desperate to change my life and do what was truly best for me, I sought help from a healer. I had no idea what this woman did or how it worked, but I felt called to it. Self-help books and therapy weren't working, and I knew there was something more.

This healer also brought up my adoption, and she helped me connect to my origin story in a way that helped me feel into the depth of it. After just a few sessions, my consciousness drastically expanded. I could sense into all the connections of where my pain was rooted, and how it was linked to where I was stuck in life. I also felt a powerful connection to life, to something bigger than myself. Even though I was experiencing major loss and huge emotions, I felt supported and safe enough to feel it all. The pressure of perfection melted away, and for the first time in my life, I felt whole.

I saw clearly how my relationship with Sienna mirrored the dynamic I shared with my birth mother. The push-pull of "I want you." "I don't want you." was a pattern that started when my mother gave me away, then wanted me back, then gave me away again. It repeated all over again with Sienna. Between the clarity I had and all of the soul-level healing I'd done, I was able to walk away from Sienna.

In the year that followed, my life changed in unimaginable ways, yet again. I found out who my birth mother was. I met the love of my life. I lost my best friend, my mom, to cancer. I felt safe to grieve and feel the full spectrum and depth of my emotions. And when my healer suggested I pursue becoming a healer myself, I said "yes" to the call to help people on the deepest soul level.

As children, we depend on our mothers for survival. When children's physical and emotional needs aren't met, they believe it's their fault, and they'll go to great lengths to "fix themselves" to attain love and safety. This is how mother wounds form. Most of our mother wounds take root in the gaps where the core needs we had as children were not consistently met. The good news is that you have the power to meet those needs of your inner child, and this is where deep healing takes place.

Anytime I was struggling, felt stuck or fearful, I'd sit down and pinpoint which unmet core need was triggering me. These core needs vary in every person and include:

Being seen
Being heard
Being nurtured and comforted, physically and emotionally
Having your emotions validated
Feeling safe
Having time and permission to play
The freedom to create and explore your unique interests
Structure and gentle discipline
Open communication

Once I knew which unmet need I was dealing with, I would find ways I could now meet that need for my inner child. What helped most was reminding "little me" that I was now safe, that I would always be with her, and that it was more than okay for her to make mistakes (and we could have fun doing so). Other options include:

Giving regular affirmations to my inner child:
"You are safe with me."
"It's okay to be scared, and I'm here for you."

"I am so proud of you."

Creating fun activities for my inner child and me to do together:
Playing a sport I loved as a child
Arts and crafts
Having a consistent bedtime
Nourishing myself with a healthy meal
Curling up in a soft blanket and reading a book
Asking my inner child how she's doing.

The key is using these practices consistently. I was intentional about having these conversations and engaging with my inner child several times a week. By doing this over time, deep healing occurred and my childhood wounds transformed.

My mother wounds run deep. They're at the root of my extreme perfectionism. They're at the heart of my fear of abandonment. It's what made me fear and avoid my emotions for over thirty years. When I finally faced them and gave myself the time and space to heal, I was able to give and receive **real** love and found the freedom to be who I was born to be.

Fourteen

Awaken

Accepting God's Plan Through Faith

ANNA BERENDS

My parents' upbringing was tough, just like mine. The generational trauma for both of them continued, not because they wanted it to but because they didn't know how to stop it. Dad was tough and at times miserable. Mom struggled through the days, fighting between depression, anxiety and her own misery, making it difficult to parent.

We lived in the same house for eighteen years, I was far more afraid of dad than I would like to admit. Anxiety was my constant companion. Strangely, if you were to ask me if I would choose to be raised in the same home all over again, I would say 'yes' because they are my family and I love them. I have a wonderful sister that is smart, beautiful and full of inspiration.. My older brother is emotional and eccentric, his circle is small, but his love is big. My youngest brother has a tough exterior covered in tattoos, and at times a foul mouth, but that's just to cover up his soft heart. He'd give the shirt off his back to help someone out.

My family wasn't perfect, not even close, family life was layered with good and bad. On the exterior we looked like any other family. Our lives were filled with school, church activities, sports and playing with friends. Intermingled in those hard times were family camping trips in the summer to Seaside, Oregon. Dad could be found behind the camera as we played on the beach. The ocean waves crashed against the sand and begged to be played in. The salty breeze would settle on my tongue and blow strands of my hair across my face. The smell of deep fried corn dogs and elephant ears would pull me off Broadway street. I could hear the screams and laughter of children from the Funland Entertainment Center.

My eyes moved quickly through the space being drawn to the disco ball and bright flashes of red, green and white light. The tilt-o-whirl was my favorite. My heart would race with anticipation as I stood in line.

Am I going to die this time? I said to myself, as I watched the tiny wheels spin in circles under the ride. *How could they possibly keep it in place?*

My turn would soon come; my legs felt like rubber as I walked to the ride. I took my seat and looked up as the safety bar came over my head. My heart thumped in my chest as my hands gripped the bar. The ride moved side to side and whipped in circles as my breath would catch and my stomach ached from the laughter that traveled blocks away. I would want to go again, over and over. The muffled sound of the M.C., loud music, and bumper cars hovered in the air as I tried to take it all in. As I looked at my siblings' faces, I could see how happy they were and thought, *This is perfect.*

Dad was a different person here. *I love to see him laugh and smile,* I thought while he would joke and play, something that wasn't seen all that often at home.

My parents had a whirlwind courtship, meeting in the spring of 1979 and were married in July of that year. In the five years that followed, my three siblings and I were born. One can only imagine the pandemonium that must have taken place and the insurmountable stress that put on both of my parents. Dad tirelessly worked as a salesman, sometimes gone for days while on the road. In my adult years, Mom would say that was a godsend because having Dad home only made things more challenging for her. Mom was home among dirty diapers, nap times that didn't go as planned, doctors appointments, grocery shopping, and disorganized meal times. *Sesame Street* could be heard playing on the TV while Mom would try to get away to pick up the house or put in a load of laundry. A shower was on the to do list, as well, but was always pushed to the bottom of a never-ending list of chores and children who needed attention.

Mom was raised in a Latter Day Saint household and Dad, as I understand it, did not attend church on a regular basis. Within a year of being married in my great-grandparent's backyard, Dad was baptized a member of the Church of Jesus Christ of Latter Day Saints, and later they were sealed in the Seattle Temple. Life would later prove difficult as my parents both had different ideas of a happy life; their arguments frequent and normal. Mom promised Heavenly Father that she would keep her marriage together no matter what and in doing so, tried to control Dad's every move. Dad would escape whenever he could just to feel free from the oppression at home.

The financial strain of living in Des Moines, Washington, became too heavy and when I was five my family moved to Yakima. The dad that I grew to know would put on a front in the presence of people, not wanting to let anyone into his truth. As I got older, I can remember him saying, *"Jones business is Jones business."* In other words, keep your mouth shut.

I was never good at being silenced. During my teens years, I realized that being criticized (mostly for my weight), belittled, manipulated, and screamed at wasn't normal. *I can't do anything right*, would cross my mind often after getting in his way.

My freshman year of high school was an absolute nightmare. With no self esteem and no friends, I preferred my own company to that of my peers.

The most terrifying memory I have of my parents arguing came in April of that year and ended with Dad being taken away in an ambulance. I knew far more about my parents' marriage than anyone in their teen years would want to know. Mom told me all the things, and not knowing any better and wanting to help her, I listened and gave her advice I had no business giving.

In the summer of 1995 and with hope for a new beginning, we moved to Utah without Dad. The drive was long and tedious. While riding in the car I heard the name *April*, whispered in my ear and thought *that was strange*. I paused my Walkman, took off my headphones and looked around the car only to see that everyone was sleeping except for me. I waited a couple more minutes. Nothing came.

The day after we arrived in South Jordan, Utah, a knock came at the door of my aunt and uncle's home. "*It's for you*," my uncle said. *For me?*

"*Hello, I'm Julie and this is my daughter, April.*" I stood there in astonishment, staring at the girl with the most beautiful red hair, trying not to make a bad impression, but the previous day's voice came back to me.

Did she just say that her daughter's name is April? It's not possible, but it was. Julie invited my sister and I to girls camp. *No way*, I thought, *nuh-uh*. We had just moved to Utah and didn't know anyone.

April and I were the same age, our birthdays only four days apart. We became the greatest of friends and spent countless hours together that summer, including girls camp, and in the next four years. The Christlike example of her family and the time spent with them over the years still influences me. They took me into their home and showed me what family and love looked like.

At the beginning of my sophomore year, she introduced me to her friend group. My insecurities of the previous years and having no friends flooded my mind and with trepidation, I thought, *I hope they like me!* Then there was Jake, his goofy nature, the way he could make me laugh and his not-so serious approach to life drew me to him. He was always there for advice or a good laugh. My friend group continued to grow over the next few years and has lasted into adulthood.

After high school I watched my friends as they went off to college or married. I stumbled through life, left the church of Jesus Christ of Latter-Day Saints, and made choices that led myself and others to heartache. In 2006 I married a non-member. Shortly after our marriage I realized that I had a testimony of the gospel and wanted to return to church. I missed the people, the hymns, the ability to connect with members, and to be able to bear my testimony of Jesus. I couldn't go to church activities, have members or missionaries in the home or read the Book of Mormon. In our first year of marriage our daughter Morgan arrived, and so did the arguments. My attempts to return to the church were met with anger and hostility.

In the following years my prayers were answered and we were blessed with two more children, Olive and Milo, after having five miscarriages. My spouse and I began to grow apart. We stopped talking and we would have yelling matches often, neither one being heard. The love was gone, and yet I didn't want to admit we had failed–I had failed. We divorced quickly and in the following months I became severely depressed. I lost my home, family, my belongings and missed having the kids around. I watched another family form with my kids and without me. I had moved into a different county and felt so removed from their lives. We shared custody of the kids but it still felt empty. My darkest moment came on a phone call with the suicide hotline. I was desperate for the pain to stop, for me to be able to feel like I could breathe again. The party on the other side of the phone advised me to make a choice about my life. I knew I didn't want to be gone from their lives forever.

I made a difficult choice and moved four hours away. **I left my kids**. A choice that ultimately saved my life but hurt my children deeply. Over the next eight years, I drove up and down the freeway between Wisconsin and Minnesota to pick them up for weekend visits that went all too quickly. Sadness and I were best friends and I often cried.

I met Cory in the summer of 2017. He showed me that I could be loved as he helped me pick up the pieces of my life. We fought for my kids through the court system but lost every time. I didn't think I was going to ever have custody of them again.

I made many attempts to return to the church, but it was not as I remembered. I felt like an outsider, an imposter. I did not want to align my life with gospel principles and give up the parts of my life that brought me happiness.

The awakening came as I realized that worldly happiness is fleeting and I needed my Savior. I hit my knees and cried out to Jesus for help. Life had become too hard, my soul felt empty and trying to fill it with the world had left me alone, I felt like I was drowning. In desperation and with a prompting from the Holy Ghost, I called the missionaries. Elder Child and Elder Moala came over that night. My road back to church was difficult; I held on to what I used to know and began to feel my Savior's love for me grow. My knowledge of the gospel returned as I aligned my life with gospel principles, and the spirit of Christ filled my home once again.

Life would come to an abrupt halt with the diagnosis of a serious illness, and the realization that Dad may not be around much longer. I was flooded with emotions including anger. I was mad at myself and mad at him. Living states away I felt cheated out of a father-daughter relationship. I know he is far from youth at seventy-three, but I found myself wanting to go back in time. To do it all over again. So that he would know that he is capable of love and that I loved him, even through the hurt. All I could do was trust that God's plan is always better than mine. I'm not ready for there to just be memories. As an adult I want to go back in time for him and give him what he so desperately wanted and needed as a child. Love. Then maybe it could have been different. We could have had a different story.

Today my parents have been divorced for twenty-five years. Dad is pretty quiet about his illness so we talk about life, dreams, art projects, what we read, and family. Mom has always been close by; she comes over for Sunday dinners and family time. Many of the struggles I have encountered as an adult have been similar to the ones that my father went through, bringing a new perspective to my life. My lens on life is different now, requiring me to try harder not to judge myself or others. We may never know what someone is going through or how to help them, but we can offer a kinder response to their struggle. A smile, a phone call, a text message, and even a simple 'hello' to the person on the street may be all they need to feel seen and loved. Living in the moment has never been more important to me as my children are growing, making life choices and looking for guidance. After Dad passes I will choose to remember him living in the moment, behind the camera, laughing and smiling, as my siblings and I played on the beach.

I have been truly blessed as I follow the example of my Savior, our Savior. Cory and I are happily married and have custody of my children–our life is full of love, laughter and family.

God moved mountains and Jesus showed me that forgiveness is possible. I had to forgive myself and relinquish control and make a conscious choice to let God in. To not let what happened to me, or the choices that I made still define me. I knew that I needed the atonement now more than ever. I became aware that our Father in Heaven's love is ever reaching and it was never kept from me, even when I felt alone. The love of Jesus healed me to my soul as I gave up control. God put people in my path who I needed, over and over, answering my prayers. I can promise you that the love of Jesus is there for you if you open your heart to him. He knows you and your pain. You can heal!

Fifteen

Broken Childhood

How I Became A Cycle-Breaking Mom

JACQUELYNN POWERS

I thought I had come to terms with my absolute shitty child-hood.

I had done therapy on my own and with my mom. I had practiced Kundalini yoga, read self-help books, and pretty much lived by the mantra, "That what doesn't kill you makes you stronger."

I had come to a place where I credited my trauma for making me tough, independent and successful.

I was good. Or so I thought.

Until I had my first child and I held this tiny little creature in my arms and marveled at how soft she was. How sweet. How small. How she smelled like a vanilla cupcake. My husband would wrap her in his T-shirt during her first week. She was that petite.

The bliss was short-lived because caring for this pink and perfect little girl made me question my own childhood. How could my own mother hit me? How could anyone harm something this helpless, which they had created, and their only job was to nurture and protect?

Why did she abuse me throughout my childhood? Why did she torture me with a hairbrush, running it through my hair so violently that I ran away from her, preferring knots and matted tufts to the shiny, tangle-free hair like my classmates in kindergarten?

Why did she tell me I was an accident and she had seriously contemplated having an abortion?

Why did I have to carry family secrets? Why did we move so often? Why did my parents come home so late from nightclubs and sleep all day? Why did my egg salad have pieces of shell in it?

How I envied other children and their stable lives.

When I was in my twenties, I gathered a few answers. My mom and I went to therapy and I learned about her trauma. During that process, I understood three things: One, she had been abused by her mother. Two, she was addicted to a range of pills over the years that spanned copious amounts of quaaludes, Valium, and Oxycontin. Three, she was in a codependent relationship with a fellow addict—my father—and she hit me to get his attention.

None of that made me feel any better. Quite the opposite because if she had suffered from abuse, why would she continue the cycle?

Nevertheless, we came to an uneasy truce. I still harbored resentment and I didn't trust her, but we were able to coexist amicably for many years. Like polite strangers who were somehow related.

The detente worked—until I had my first child.

When my daughter was born, the Post Traumatic Stress Disorder (PTSD) I had stuffed so far into the depths of my core came roaring out. I was so angry. Furious. Incredulous. Frankly, pissed off.

I couldn't look at my mother.

I didn't want her near me or my baby, which was pretty much fine by her. She wasn't comfortable around babies. She put on a show if other people were around, patting my daughter's head like she was a dog, but otherwise zoning out with her phone or walking outside for a cigarette.

The biggest reckoning was with my father, though. How could he allow this abuse to happen?

Of course, he had been beaten too. Hitting your child as a form of discipline was pretty much a given back in the 1950s. My father was wild, the child of two survivors of the Holocaust who were working backbreaking jobs and long hours to support their new life in America. Neglected by default, he got in trouble at school often and was harshly punished.

Clearly, generational trauma courses through my DNA on both sides of my family tree.

However, I had always thought of my father as my hero, my savior. When my mother hit me, he would take me for ice cream or shopping sprees. Once, we ran away to Disney World for the weekend, just the two of us. We had a song we used to sing, "We love each other, not the mother."

When I was an adult, my father and I worked together for twenty years building a publishing empire I was so proud of. We were a team—or so I thought.

He spoiled me with money and gifts. When he sold the magazine, my father helped me buy a home. He even paid for my car and health insurance until I was forty. All this was to assuage his guilt and keep me in his orbit because he knew that one day I would connect the dots.

While he never hit me, my father was fully aware of what was going on with my mother and never did anything to stop the abuse. Perhaps that is even worse.

It only took me forty-two years to realize he was just as culpable as she was.

I'll never forget when I called one of my best friends, who was in the Traumatic Childhood Club too, and explained my newfound epiphany about my father. Her reaction? "Finally!" she shouted.

I'm embarrassed to admit I didn't see it or didn't want to see it because unconsciously I couldn't handle it. I wasn't as strong as I thought.

However, having kids gave me Hulk-sized strength. I became a mama bear overnight. Unfuckable with.

During the first week home with my baby, I made a major life decision: I was going to end the cycle of abuse in my family line. My children would never flinch in fear of being hit by an open hand or a sharp belt. Abuse would be a concept so foreign to them they couldn't even fathom it.

I created family rules, as opposed to the family secrets I grew up with, and number one was that we don't hit. Anyone. Ever.

No punching, kicking, scratching, or biting either. While they were toddlers, I repeated the no hitting rule ad nauseam.

"We don't hit in this family," was a constant motto.

Certainly, there were a few incidents in preschool. I over-apologized to the mom whose daughter was bitten by mine. I felt a sense of shame, but the mom—and school—reassured me this was normal behavior.

My son had a bully when he was four years old. I taught him to advocate for himself but never to hit anyone. Thankfully, my son is a pretty chill dude, so I don't worry too much about fights.

As my children get older, I have shared bits and pieces of my childhood with them. Trauma watered down. They understand that grandma hit me and how that was wrong.

Sometimes my daughter stares at me wide-eyed when I discuss my childhood. It's a fine line for me to walk. I don't want to terrify my children and I don't want their pity. Instead, I want them to understand the collateral damage.

My husband tells me to move on, that was all in the past, no one wants to hear these stories. "Why do you keep bringing it up?" he asks?

But I deployed those evasive tactics for too long. I kept my family secrets, and it ate me up inside. I was bitter and broken but wasn't self-aware enough to realize it was affecting every part of my life—from drinking too much and dating the wrong men.

I want to do better for my children. I need to. I prayed for children for so long, and I know they are a precious gift. For at least eighteen years, I serve as their guardian, protector, safety net, and example.

I'm not perfect. I've made a lot of mistakes along the way.

I have yelled at my kids, more often than I care to admit. Whether it was during the Covid-19 pandemic, and I hadn't had a break in months, or due to the constant whining, which drives me crazy.

I immediately apologize after I lose my temper. I explain to them that mommy should have handled the situation more calmly, and I am trying to do better every day.

Despite all the trauma and drama, I've never hit my children—and I never will.

As for my parents, our relationship was never the same after I had children. In fact, we went months without speaking because I needed to clear my head and keep the space where I was raising my children safe. Just because you are related to someone doesn't mean they have to be in your life. It's healthy to step away.

However, around the time my daughter was born, my father was diagnosed with stage four colon cancer. He had lost so much weight and was weak and damaged from the ravaging disease and subsequent chemotherapy and radiation treatments. He was also pretty much broke—and broken.

It was heartbreaking to watch.

My mother, who had always lived in her own world, retreated further into fantasy land and denial. She was alive, but barely.

The next few years were a blur of taking care of two children born a year apart, dealing with my parents' deteriorating situation, political chaos, a global pandemic, and ultimately their back-to-back deaths.

I was overwhelmed, stressed out and barely sleeping. My friends asked how I was carrying on with so much upheaval and adversity. The answer? I was a mother and my children were my first priority.

Motherhood fits me like a glove. It feels natural and pure. Where there was anger and resentment before, there is now just love. I feel lighter because I broke the generational trauma that has run through my family for so long. It weighed heavily on me in so many ways. However, I did have closure when my father passed away. I was with him for his last days of hospice and forgave him. It was healing for me to let the past go.

I parent gently, the way I wish I had been treated. I'm firm when needed and set boundaries around important things. Like the no hitting rule or always being kind. I probably let my kids eat too much ice cream and buy them too many Squishmallows, but it fills me with joy to see them happy.

I hug my kids all the time and tell them how much they are wanted and how loved they are. While I encourage them to spend time with their friends or pursue their interests, I am trying to build a strong foundation of love first. When they do fly free, they will establish their own relationships based on love and trust.

HONORING MY INNER CHILD

One of the most challenging times I face as a survivor of childhood abuse is when I am brushing my daughter's hair. This simple act triggers my inner child because this was often when my mother was most violent.

My mom's wrath was taken out on me and my knotty hair. How I feared the brush. Long tresses often matted. Screaming, "No, please don't brush my hair. Stop, you're hurting me."

It felt like torture. No care was taken. It was done with malicious intent.

When you do healing work, a lot of it centers around re-parenting your inner child. Visualizing yourself in these situations but with love. You can go back and softly brush your inner child's hair. Tell her it will be okay. Send love to the terrified mini you once were.

My daughter has beautiful long hair. Golden locks, which also get tangled. It's a much longer process to take care of it properly. To work out the knots that weave their way into Florida kids' hair by way of the powerful sun, damaging pool water, and pieces of seaweed from the ocean. Don't even get me started on slime.

It would be much faster to rip a brush through her knotted hair. It takes much longer to moisturize it with a leave-in detangler. To lovingly brush through each section. To gently coax out the tangles. But this is what I do. For my daughter and for myself.

ROLE PLAYING

Another parenting hack I invented is a game I like to call, "What would my mom do?" Then I do the opposite.

When I'm getting my kids dressed for school in the morning and we're inevitably running late, I might find that my daughter's shorts have a small hole in it or that my son's favorite T-shirt is stained.

For a moment, I think it's fine. The T-shirt is only going to get dirty at school. Why bother?

But then, I ask myself, "What would my mother do in this situation?" Since I know the answer, I do the complete opposite, which means the T-shirt goes in the laundry and the shorts go in the trash.

This system never fails me, but then again, I had a really toxic role model.

VISUALIZING THE FUTURE

Parenthood is not easy! Even Mother Teresa would have her hands full with whining, crying, melting-down toddlers. Sometimes I'm so touched-out as a mom, I want to run away for a few hours. Privacy? It doesn't exist when you're a mom—not even in the bathroom.

When I get overwhelmed, I visualize our future. Being tuned into advice from my future self, some call it intuition, has been a game changer for me. I picture my kids as teenagers or even adults. They won't want to hold my hand anymore or ask me to make cookies with them. Their problems will be grown up and challenging.

There's an expression in parenting that says, "The days are long but the years are quick." It's true. A rainy weekend with no plans can feel like an eternity. But then you blink and the kids are in elementary school and turning ten.

The first time I was truly touched-out and my son wanted to hold my hand, I started to pull away. Then this inner voice clearly spoke to me and said, "One day soon you will wish you could still hold his hand." So I leaned into it and cherished the moment.

Another time my son asked me to walk him into class and sit with him for a few minutes. This went on for a full week. He had been terri-fied by a scene in a movie where the mother was killed and he wanted me with him. Late for work? Yup. But I did what felt right because be-ing there for my child was more important.

I am a proud cycle breaker, ending generations of abuse and trauma.

Sixteen

Healing After the Memory Fades

A Daughter's Journey of Healing

MANDY BARR

The baby monitor crackled to life with my mom's faint yet urgent call.

"Mandy, Mandy, I need you!"

The sound pierced through my exhausted slumber, yanking me back to the harsh reality of caregiving. My eyes felt gritty from lack of sleep, my muscles ached, and my brain swam in a fog. Money was tight, and we couldn't afford overnight caretakers anymore. Almost every night, I found myself changing her sheets and showering her because she wet the bed despite wearing adult diapers.

Alzheimer's pursued like a relentless beast, and her condition had been deteriorating at a fast pace. Each day was a new struggle, but I refused to let it break me. I found strength amid the chaos.

I threw the covers off and stumbled out of bed, my mind screaming, *What the fuck was I thinking?* Just six months into my marriage with
Dave and in the middle of a global pandemic, I had moved my mom
in with us. My childhood friends were shocked to learn I made this
decision.

From a young age, I could feel the sting of my mother's resentment
whenever she called me "little dick." It wasn't just a nickname but a
reflection of her deep-seated jealousy. I was my father's pride and joy,
his "daddy's little girl," and she hated that I repeatedly chose him over
her. My father, Richard, understood me in ways she never could.

"Amanda, you can be anything you want in life; you just need to
put your mind and effort towards it."

Although my father and grandfather, who we called poppy, wanted
me to be an independent woman, my mother and grandmother
wanted me to stay close to home and marry a nice man who would
care for me. In their mind, my ultimate job was to care for my mother
when she aged, and they made no qualms about discussing this with
everyone.

On the other hand, my father and poppy encouraged me to pursue
my dreams and supported my aspirations, which often clashed with
my mother and grandmother's expectations.

I'll never forget visiting with my grandparents soon after my college graduation and discussing my career plans.

With a sharp tongue, my grandmother said, "Amanda, I helped pay
for college so you could find a husband."

With a quick volley back, my poppy said, "Clara, she is a career
woman."

But that wasn't the biggest issue. I was just like my father—gre-
garious, sarcastic, and full of life. My mother resented me as much as
she resented her marriage to him, seeing in me all the qualities she
felt overshadowed by and trapped in. Her bitterness was a constant
presence in my childhood, a shadow that marred the light my father

brought into my life. So, caring for my mom was never on my bucket list of things to do in my lifetime.

I pulled myself together and ran down the stairs, my heart pounding with dread. I found her on the floor, having fallen, trying to get up. She was dead weight, and lifting her alone was impossible.

I shouted, "Dave! I need help!"

He came rushing in, finding us both in a sorry state. My mom was soaked, the sheets were torn from the bed, and my lip was bleeding from biting down so hard to keep from crying.

Something was different this morning. Mom seemed even more confused and disoriented than usual. She couldn't follow even the simplest of directions. After much struggle, we managed to get her cleaned up, and her bed changed, and we began our typical morning routine.

Each morning, she sat on the couch to eat breakfast while watching *The View*. We placed a little folding table before her for her morning feast. However, I couldn't get her upright, and her face on one side looked slightly droopy.

Panic gripped me. *Shit, did she have another mini-stroke?*

Mom was blessed with both vascular dementia and Alzheimer's, which confused many of us. Her symptoms didn't follow the typical Alzheimer's pattern; she wasn't recalling memories from the past, and she had lost her ability to write. Her vocabulary was also slipping away rapidly. Watching her beautiful script handwriting turn into an unreadable chicken scratch was particularly hard for me.

Despite our differences, she used to write me notes and leave them in my lunch bag. *Have a wonderful day, my beautiful daughter.* I wish I still had one of those notes to look at today.

It wasn't until we connected with a neurologist and had a functional magnetic resonance imaging (fMRI) scan done that we got a detailed look at mom's brain. Sure enough, there were clear signs of both Alzheimer's and vascular dementia. As the doctor pointed out the areas of her brain affected by mini-strokes, I realized each one had caused a portion of her memory to die. While I was overwhelmed by the results, a part of me felt relief—*Finally, there was proof of what was happening to her.*

Alzheimer's is a trickster, sometimes making you think your loved one has a mood disorder, which I had suspected in Mom's case anyway. Despite this, she was never formally diagnosed, to the best of my knowledge.

"Mom, honey, sit up straight to eat breakfast." I fixed her posture, and she would slouch over again. I looked to Dave for guidance.

"Something's not right."

One of the things I will never forget about mom is her love for food, especially food made for her, just as she liked it. Every morning, it was oatmeal with two shakes of cinnamon, one-half cup of milk, a healthy squeeze of honey, two slices cinnamon raisin toast with a light smear of butter, black coffee with one sweetener packet, and a cup of orange juice with low acid, no pulp. Only on the weekends after church did we defer from this menu. We would eat breakfast at Eli's, and she would get waffles with whipped cream, strawberries, and well-done bacon. As her condition worsened, she lost her appetite and the joy she once found in her favorite meals, which was heartbreaking for me to witness.

I did the only thing I could think of—I called Carolan Gozzi, my neighbor and the older sister I never had. Carolyn had been a rock for me, offering advice on how to be a good wife, a better mom, and, now, how to care for an aging parent. She was at my door within minutes, bringing a wave of relief. She knew the graphic and gory details of my life with my mom, and she never judged me for my doubts or frustrations.

Carolan looked at me and then at Mom.

"Marilyn. Hi, Marilyn, wow, look at that breakfast. That looks delicious, darling." She spoke to her sweet and encouragingly, but Mom responded little to nothing.

"Marilyn, are you hungry, sweetheart?"

Mom still did not respond. You see, my mom and Carolan had formed a special connection. My mother loved the energy of the Gozzis family. Their children were always out and about, which made Mom so happy. Her not responding to Carolan was further evidence that something was wrong.

Turning back to look at me, she said, "You know what you need to do."

Tears welled in my eyes as I nodded, understanding the gravity of her words.

Within moments, the Natick fire department and police were there, shining a flashlight in her eyes and trying to get her to talk.

I could vaguely hear and see what was happening. I felt like I was watching the scene unfold from above, detached from my body.

"Mandy, they need to know where to take her."

Carolan's words bring me back to reality. Looking at the Emergency Medical Technician,

"Newton Wellesley Hospital."

As they started wheeling mom out on a stretcher, she finally responded to what was happening, bursting into tears, so confused. "Mandy, what's happening? Where am I going?"

"It's ok, momma. They are taking you to the hospital to get checked out. I will be right behind you in my car."

"Please, I'm scared."

"I know, momma, you are safe and in excellent hands. I'll see you so soon you won't have time to miss me."

As the ambulance doors closed, reality hit me like a freight train. "Oh my God, she's not coming home again."

That day, January 27, 2023, marked the end of an era.

The following days were a blur of hospital visits and endless paperwork. We faced heart-wrenching decisions about her care. Should she receive assistance with breathing or eating? Should we try to resuscitate her if she stops breathing? My head spun with uncertainty. *Have we ever discussed these things?* I knew what my dad would have wanted, but she had never told me her wishes. Despite the fog of confusion, I felt sure she wouldn't want machines keeping her alive. Yet, the thought of not resuscitating her felt unbearable.

Dave held my hand through it all, his presence a steady anchor in the storm. Carolan checked in on me daily, and her support was unwavering.

In the hospital, doctors confirmed my fears. Though they couldn't be entirely sure, they were confident that mom had suffered another stroke in addition to contracting Covid-19 for the first time. The combination left her even more debilitated, accelerating her condition at a rapid pace. It felt as though, in the blink of an eye, she had progressed to the advanced stages of her disease, which she had.

I spent hours by her bedside, holding her hand and talking to her, even though she often didn't respond. Each blank stare and mumbled word made my heart ache. I felt the weight of every unspoken word and lost connection, my love for her unwavering despite the distance her illness had created between us.

The five days she was in the hospital, I was sure she was going to die. While I had seen my mom sick, weak, and failing, I never doubted her resolve to fight back and come to the other side. However, this time felt different.

At the end of each day, I would leave the hospital and come home, heading straight to the laundry room. There, I would collapse on the floor, rocking back and forth, crying the ugliest, most gut-wrenching cry imaginable. Memories of our life flooded my mind: childhood holidays, my awkward adolescence, teenage arguments about my friends and the boys I dated, and the pride in her eyes at my graduation from high school and college.

I remembered the milestones of young adulthood, my marriage, entering motherhood, and, of course, my divorce, the period of my life where I was shattered into a thousand pieces, and she helped me put it back together, piece by piece. And, of course, our most recent memories of her living with us are the closest to my heart.

Amidst those memories were the small, cherished handwritten notes she used to leave in my lunch bags. The last note she wrote was for my son, Michael, and me during one of our trips to Connecticut after Michael's father and I separated. During those first few summers, we made countless trips to visit her, spending time at the beach during the day and grilling at night. She always packed us snacks for the ride back to Boston, a simple gesture filled with love and care.

"I love you both and have cherished these weekends together."

An unmistakable wave of gratitude struck me. Realizing she did her best, I remembered what my bonus mom told me, "She was the best mother she knew how to be."

At that moment, I didn't know what the future held, whether she would live or not, but I understood that despite her harsh words, coldness, and anger, there were countless loving things my mother had done for me.

Today, I get to choose gratitude and focus on those beautiful memories—the times she stood by my side and fought for me, the moments she told me she was proud of me, the times she bailed me out of jackpots before my divorce and every time she told me, "If you're happy, then I am happy."

It takes grit and tenacity to remember the good during difficult times, to stay open and full of love, and to practice gratitude for everything, even the messy and imperfect. Allowing yourself to remain open makes you vulnerable, which can be scary. It's much easier to build walls around your heart and memories, fabricating stories to protect yourself. However, doing so means missing out on the magic of life and the beauty all around you.

A daily gratitude practice has been transformative for me. It helped heal my heart and enabled me to forgive my mom for her imperfections. This forgiveness has allowed us to develop a relationship I never dreamed possible, all because I chose to change my perspective.

Mom did survive and now lives in a nursing home in Waltham. I still sometimes retreat to the laundry room for a good, ugly cry because watching the progression of this disease is monstrous. Each decline rips away another level of her dignity. She is primarily non-verbal, unable to eat or drink on her own, and entirely dependent on others to move her from bed to wheelchair.

She lost her ability to walk about six months after that hospital visit. I continued to advocate for her to have more physical and occupational therapy, as well as be given additional assistive devices to help her eat.

Eventually, the medical team told me, "We've done all we can."

While I am grateful that she remembers me most days, there are times when she struggles, especially if I haven't visited for a few days. Eventually, her memory returns, and she will proudly exclaim, "I remember now."

I smile and touch her face. "I know, momma."

Caring for my mom was never something I planned, but it taught me invaluable lessons about strength, sacrifice, gratitude, service, and unconditional love. Despite the hardships, it allowed us to heal and connect deeply, forging the special mother-daughter relationship we both longed for.

As we begin to plan for hospice care, I also prepare for my future, a process filled with both excitement and grief. Over the last four-plus years, I have sacrificed so much, but I have also gained a deeper understanding of myself and my capacity for love and resilience.

Now, it's time to step back into my life, to rebuild and rediscover who I am beyond being a caregiver. Daily gratitude and a heart to serve will remain my guiding principles as I navigate this new chapter.

Seventeen

Mom's Time In

The Truth Will Set You Free

THEA SOMMER

My sons were nineteen months apart. Jeremy was twenty-three months old and Benny forty-two months old. I was going through a brutal part of my divorce and running my own business.

Standing at the refrigerator on a Sunday morning, I handed Jeremy his sippy cup of apple juice. He threw it on the floor. My jaws clenched.

"Pick that up" I said.

He screamed, "No! Red."

In the calmest voice I could muster, that sing-song voice I hoped would calm him the hell down, I said, "Oh, ok, you want the red top on your sippy cup?"

Opening the cabinet of sippy cups, plastic dishes, and lids, I pulled out a red one and changed it out. I handed it to Jeremy. He threw it and I lost it.

Like I really lost it. The kind of crying and yelling that we all do and don't tell anyone about because we're so ashamed...that's what I was doing. "Here, take it, here!"

Jeremy started crying; Benny looked up from the TV in the family room, and I kept yelling. Jeremy kept crying; Benny came running over—both of them staring at me. I knew they were scared, and I kept yelling. I knew what I was doing wasn't right, and I kept yelling. Benny started crying and did his best to not show it, and I kept yelling.

Then I stopped. I leaned against the fridge, slid down, and just started sobbing.

"I'm sorry, I'm so sorry, Mommy's so sorry."

I held my arms out; they each fell into me, the three of us crying. "It's okay Mommy, it's okay," Benny said.

"No Benny, it isn't okay."

My sanity was returning, and I knew that while I wanted my sons to understand that we all mess up and it's good to forgive, I didn't want them to learn that kind of aggressive behavior is acceptable no matter how bad things are.

Benny said, "You're right. I hate you when you yell."

My tears stopped. "What did you say?"

My oldest boy, all of three-and-a-half years old, looked me right in the eyes and with precision he slowly and clearly said, "I hate you when you yell. Get it?"

I was astounded. I thought, *How could he possibly say that to me?* Immediately following, *He is amazing and brave.* Two opposing thoughts equally impacted me.

"Benny, you are right. I don't like myself when I yell either. I'm going to be better."

I hugged my boys. We wiped our tears on my T-shirt, drank our juice, ate our breakfast, and prepared for the day.

Six hours later the three of us were at the park for yet another birthday party. Jeremy's friend from school, Cameron, was turning two. Most of the kids went to school together, so there was a clique of moms who had to go to those parties. We mostly hung out because at two and three years old, it wasn't really fair to just drop them off.

Cindy had just had her second baby, Charlie. Her older daughter and Jeremy were the same age. As the four of us stood in the shade just blabbing, Cindy was holding Charlie doing the mom rock with him on her shoulder.

"Can I hold him?" I asked.

Before she could say absolutely, she handed him to me. I smelled his hair and watched him breathe and went right into the mom rock.

"Oh, my goodness, they are so yummy at this age" I said softly.

"Yes," Cindy said. "Until you can't shut him up at 3 a.m., and then I want to throw him out the window."

The other three of us kind of cracked up, but definitely with caution. Then Melissa, one of the other moms said, "You can't believe what Emma did the other day!"

Emma was also in school with Jeremy and Cindy's daughter. We looked at her already smiling.

Melissa said, "All I wanted to do was go to the freakin' bathroom to pee. I came out and Emma had my red Chanel lipstick and had drawn all over herself and my white couch!"

As a side note, who has a white couch when you have kids? But I digress.

Melissa continued, "I picked Emma up and put her outside in the yard."

Cindy asked, "Why? So, you could hose her off?"

Melissa's response was hysterical. "No! So, I wouldn't throw her out the window!"

That was it. We were laughing so hard our stomachs hurt, and we couldn't stop. And then we'd stop and look at each other and start cracking up all over again.

I stopped laughing. My laughter tears turned to the sad ones, and I said, "I had a really tough morning—really, really tough."

They looked at me with so much concern and love—yes, love. I took a breath and told them everything. Believe me, there were parts I wanted to leave out. I was so embarrassed and ashamed. I felt like a monster, but I told the whole thing. It was amazing. When I was done, they hugged me and started sharing their own harrowing stories about losing control with their kids.

That hour changed my life.

The loudest thought in my head was, We can't be the only ones. I started to think of all the moms I knew and all of the moms I didn't know. And how we all must be suffering at some level. This was over twenty years ago when there was no social media and no mom's support groups you could join online.

I decided to get ten moms I knew together. I made sure we were different in age, in the ages of our kids, in our backgrounds, some working, some not. Single moms, moms with different financial situations. All we had to have in common was being a mom.

I asked for three hours of their time, at my house, without their kids on a Sunday afternoon. That's a big ask for moms. I promised them it would be worth it. I asked that they just come ready to listen and share as honestly as they could.

I started by telling my story of that fateful day of the sippy cup. I told it with all the brutal honesty I could muster, tearing up as I recounted the experience. I then shared about the group of us at the park and those conversations. Then I asked, "Am I the only one?"

The flood gates opened. It was crazy. Giving the opportunity to share and "come clean" in a safe non-judgmental group of moms was like a golden highway to sharing all those things they had held inside, some for years. Filled with regret and pain and embarrassment, they started to share.

THE MOM'S WORKSHOP WAS BORN

And the pathway...being a mom, it's the person or people I love the most that bring something out in me that is horrific. It's terrible and I can't control it. I'm a horrible mom and a horrible person. With those ten women, we discovered that each of us had these feelings. We discovered that each of us had done things that we were too ashamed to share with anyone. And we discovered that each of us were not alone. It was part of being a mom, and no one talks about it. It's a conspiracy of secrecy. Being a mom was part of this club that had the dichotomous experience of a love so deep it's almost painful and becoming someone we didn't want to be and couldn't control. And no one talked about it.

That year I probably worked in groups with more than a hundred moms. Going into this first group, I had a sense we were all in the same place, but I didn't know why. It didn't make sense. In the fourth group of moms on a Sunday in my house, I got it. I felt like I found the key.

When we're pregnant or about to adopt a baby, everyone around us is joyous and acknowledging and takes special care of us. We walk into elevators and people smile. We're revered as the givers of the life that's growing inside of us.

And then you have your baby, and the world changes. Not just because we have this tiny thing to take care of, not because it takes everything we have, not because we're exhausted. Certainly, those things come into play.

But the real change is that all the accolades stop. People have so many expectations of us, and we have so many expectations of ourselves. We go down the deep dark cavern of it never, and I do mean never, being enough. We're not like that other mom who looks so put together; we can't stop our child from crying or throwing themselves on the floor at the grocery store. In those moments, it's really about feeling embarrassed and judged and judging ourselves. Those expectations come from our partners, our kids, our family, ourselves, and other mothers.

A major part of the glue that holds this together is that as mothers, we not only judge ourselves, but we judge each other. We're brutal in our thoughts. We don't reach out to moms whose baby is crying at the grocery store.

After that fourth group, I went shopping at a large clothing store. There was a mom there with a two-year-old, a four-year-old, and an eight-year-old. She was trying so hard to give her oldest the attention he needed to pick clothes, but her two-year-old was just two-year-old-ing to the hilt. She put the two-year-old in his stroller even though he did the "straight as a board" thing they do so you can't maneuver them—but she did it, like we all do. That baby was just screaming. Everyone in the store, seriously I could see people's eyes rolling, doing that tsk, tsk, tsk thing. Some of them were moms with their kids.

It stopped me cold.

I walked over to that mom with those three kids. I looked right at her with a little smile. I said, "It's so hard. You're doing a great job."

She teared up right there in the store. I then asked if I could help her with her two-year-old. I started smiling at him and rocking him in his stroller. He stopped crying, watching me–who knows what was going through his sweet head. Then he reached up his arms to me..."uppa, uppa."

I looked at his mom and she nodded yes. I picked that baby up, smiled at her other two kids. I stayed close to her but let her give that attention to the other kids.

She finished shopping. I had abandoned my own cart of clothes. We stood in line to check out. Some of those folks who ten minutes earlier had been tsk, tsk, tsking smiled at me and her. Some of them didn't. Some of them wouldn't even look at us.

I walked them outside. With tears in her eyes, she hugged me and said, "How can I ever thank you?"

I said, "I know exactly how. Go give another mom some love and remind her that she, like you, and like me, is a goddess."

If you're reading this and are a mom, I hope this touches your heart.

If you're having trouble, find someone to share it with. Reach down and muster the courage to be honest. Having community and support around you throughout motherhood is so valuable, but what will really set you free is telling the truth. The gasoline that fuels the car of shame, embarrassment, and guilt are the secrets we keep. That is why having a safe place to share is so important.

One way to do this is to write a letter to the person/people who may feel hurt by you. Write that letter as if no one will see it. And then, once you've written it, share it with them if you'd like. One of those letters should be to yourself and maybe to your own mom. Then reach out to other moms when they're doing great, and when they're not, remind them that they are a goddess and not a monster.

I'd be remiss if I didn't say there are some moms who do really harmful and damaging things to their children. There's no excuse or justification for that. But regardless of their past or their mental health, they too are living under that veil of impossible expectations as we all do.

Go love a mom. It'll set you free.

Eighteen

The Calm After the Storm

Navigating Your Power and Purpose

IRENE DORESTE

It's finally summer. I can shake off this school year and have some fun family time with my husband and the kids—or at least I thought I could.

We made it! As we pulled up to the dock, I started unloading the kids and the trunk full of supplies for today's adventure. You'd think we were going away for a month. The kids all raced down the weathered, rickety dock, my oldest yelling out, "The first one on the boat gets to go on the tube first!"

This started the twelfth argument of the day as they left me to carry all the towels, cooler, and supplies myself.

"Slow down!" I yelled, signaling to my husband that the kids were on their way, counting heads as they ran down the dock to make sure I still had them all. "Thanks for the help!" I shouted, just praying no one got a splinter because I forgot my tweezers.

What good is having four kids if I'm trying to carry everything from the trunk alone in one trip? I loaded up my arms and made my way down to the dock.

Not even halfway down, I could feel my arms start to burn from the weight of the cooler, towels slipping out from under my arms, and my son's cinch bag dangling around my finger, cutting off my circulation. One wrong move and this is all falling in the water.

Already exhausted from the feeding frenzy this morning, all I could think was, *Did I pack enough snacks? Do I have enough sunscreen? I wish I could see how many life jackets I had dangling off me right now. I hope I have them all.* As I stepped closer to the boat, the pain was intense, but I made it!

"Hey babe," my husband said, "Did you bring my sunglasses?"

As I shook out my arms trying to get my circulation back, I kept a loving smile on my face.

"No, I forgot them in the car. I'll go grab them. Does anyone else want anything?"

They each called out, "Yeah! Can you grab my goggles? Some water would be great. Mom, do you have my cinch bag?"

I made my way back down the scorching dock, burning the bottoms of my feet like I was walking on hot coals and sweating as if I was in hot yoga. But today is going to be a great day!

Even after the four hours of preparation this morning and the hour of traffic to get here, we are finally ready to have some fun. Only now I'm thinking, *If I could just send them all off without me, I could take a nap in the car!*

It was a crazy hot day, and the forecast was calling for some bad weather. I hate thunderstorms, but I'm sure everything will be alright. As my husband pulled the kids around on the blow-up tube attached to the back of the boat, the sun and spinning in circles had me wishing we took the kids to the movies instead. I looked up into the sky and saw dark clouds in the distance moving closer. The wind started to pick up, and I mentioned to my husband maybe it's time to head back.

"Not yet," the kids yelled. "I didn't get a chance to go on the tube yet, ma."

"The kids are having fun," my husband said. "It will be fine."

I didn't know if the pit in my stomach was telling me this wasn't a good idea or just nausea from spinning in circles all day. "One more time and we will make our way back to the dock, I promise."

I saw lightning strike in the distance. The wind was making it hard to stand while I watched the kids holding on for dear life, laughing as they whipped across the water, but I felt the wave of panic rushing through my body. "This isn't good!"

Just then the clouds opened up and the rain started pouring down, now making it hard to see my hand in front of my face, let alone my kids one-hundred feet off the boat.

"Pull them in!" I yelled to my husband.

"I'm trying," he replied.

The waves were getting bigger by the minute, the boat rocked from side to side, and the water rushed into the boat with each wave, making it impossible to keep my balance.

"We are going over!"

I had to go in and get them! In that moment, I could only hear the sound of the wind and rain swirling around me as if time had stopped and the faintest sound coming from the distance of my son's voice, "Ma, help us."

That was it. Without a second thought, I was in the water. The turbulent water was ice cold. I continued to yell out to them so they could hear the sound of my voice and know I was coming to get them. With each call out and as I got closer, my arms grew tired but my body had the adrenaline of one hundred men.

"I got you."

My two little ones grabbed me as if there was super glue attached to my body. Now looking back to see our boat turned on its side, I called out to my husband and older two to decide how to get to them.

I heard my son's voice, "We can't find dad!"

"Hang on."

With every stroke, it felt like I was pulled backward, but I finally reached them. They too latched on to me like suction cups to glass, the weight of the four of them pushing me under the water, having to pull myself back up several times. Each time I'd catch my breath and feel the sting of the saltwater burning my eyes while the rain continued to pummel us and each wave tossed us apart. My arms became numb and my adrenaline wore off. I was going under for the last time.

How am I going to save my kids when I can't even save myself?

I heard my husband's voice. I knew my kids would be safe. I heard a voice in my head telling me to just let go. As my body drifted down underneath the sea, I felt a sense of peace come over me, not a thought in my mind, just immense peace. My body drifted down to the ocean floor as I rested at the bottom for a moment, my eyes open.

I gasped for air, sitting up in my bed, my heart racing, looking around my bedroom realizing this was all a dream. The sense of peace lingered, leaving me to wonder, *Are we really okay?*

THE BREATH OF AWARENESS

This was a recurring dream that haunted me for months; something had to give. The voice inside my head telling me to just let go, surrender, you're not alone, your angels will guide you. This was the beginning of my spiritual awakening. Six years later, there are things I have learned about myself and how my angels put certain people and opportunities into my life to guide me.

Just like other parents, we want our children to be happy, joyful, and grow up to be good people, but after that night I knew something needed to change. It wasn't just my outside circumstances causing the storm; I had to look within. I had to look deeper into the paralyzing fear inside me.

Why would I get a pit in my stomach when I went to my kids' school, or feel like I was punched in the gut when someone hurt them? I took it all so personally. *They are a reflection of me*, as a parent, *I was falling short. How come I wasn't able to protect them; isn't that my job?* I was exhausted from putting everyone and everything else first. This dream was my wake-up call. I had to surrender and let go.

From what I remember, I was the kid with ants in my pants. A free spirit who probably drove my parents nuts. My grandmother actually paid me one time to sit on the couch for one hour so she could watch *Days of Our Lives*. I couldn't do it! I remember what it felt like to be the wild card, unafraid of who I was and use my voice. I was just like my mom and protective of the people I loved. I was the middle child, but my older sister and younger brother's friends all knew from a young age that if you messed with them, I was coming for you!

As a kid growing up in Queens, New York, we knew the importance of family and community. There was always a mom from the neighborhood driving around keeping a lookout. Like radar, always knowing when we were up to no good. I thought that's just what moms do.

I still have never lived down from giving my sister's friend a bloody nose at her birthday party. I think I was seven. All I needed to see was that my sister was upset and it was all over for me. Of course, I had to apologize and didn't mean a word of it and was punished for a month. I was punished a lot. That's when I started to take on the beliefs of needing to be a good girl, play nice even if others didn't; you are a re-flection of your family even if my head was about to explode; just shut up and do the right thing. But the right thing for whom?

Growing up in a Greek household, it was customary for the women to find a husband, get married, and have children. I gave up my nurs-ing career to become a good mother and wife. I watched my brilliant mother and grandmother do the same. Now, we all happen to marry loving, amazing men, but those women were my role models, the people I loved and respected the most. They made it look so easy. I saw their power as the women behind the curtain of their families, and I did the same.

The difference was I let my light and power burn out, simply falling in line. I had conditioned myself to play small, dim my light so others could shine, and shrink my personal power and voice. Even if my inner voice was telling me otherwise, I ignored it, believing that it was my role to stay in the background. I loved being a mother and devoted myself to my family, but in the process, I lost sight of who I was outside of that role. I had once been a vibrant, independent woman with passions, dreams, and a clear sense of self.

As time passed, I found myself living for everyone else—putting their needs above my own. I felt a constant pressure to fix everything, to make sure everyone was happy and safe. This expectation was one I had placed on myself, believing it was my responsibility to hold everything together.

In doing so, I poured everything I had into my family, I lost touch with myself. I was going through the motions without truly connecting to who I was or what I wanted. I became a shadow of my former self. The passion I once had was replaced with a sense of emptiness and a yearning for something more.

I knew that if I didn't change, the cost would be enormous—I would continue to spiral into a life that wasn't truly mine, a life marked by unfulfilled potential, unrealized dreams, and the loss of my authentic self. I also realized that I was modeling these same limiting beliefs to my children, unintentionally teaching them to follow in my footsteps of self-diminishment. It was in this place that my angels intervened, telling me to let go and trust they would guide me back to myself. I realized that reclaiming my light and power wasn't just important—it was essential for my survival and for living a life that was authentically mine.

THE PATH FORWARD: CHARTING A NEW COURSE

Over time, I committed to trusting the Universe to help me find myself and my true life's purpose. They brought people and opportunities into my life, and one by one, I started to embrace it all. I started studying Reiki and integrated energy therapy, and connecting and trusting my intuition, which led me down the path of self-development and transformation. With consistency and repetition, I worked to let go of all the limiting beliefs I put on myself and started living from a place of self-awareness, using emotional intelligence and nervous system regulation to help rewire my subconscious mind. By practicing these modalities, I was able to let go of old beliefs, emotional addictions, and patterns that I am no longer available for.

Living from this space gives you the opportunity to co-create your life and how you want to show up in the world. The truth is we are all drowning in our own stories. We are the only ones who hold ourselves back from living the life we want. No one else will ever have that kind of power over us unless we let them. Finding balance between parenting and personal fulfillment was a crucial turning point for me. Trusting my inner voice and knowing that the Universe can guide us through life's challenges—if you are open to it. What I have also learned from this is life doesn't happen to us, it happens for us. That's the lesson and the blessing in it all.

We all want the best for our children, but they all have their own paths to walk in this lifetime. We can't always run to their rescue. Experiencing failure, disappointment, heartache, and even betrayal is part of life. We don't have to fix anything. Our role as parents is to model and stand in our unique wholeness as the pillar of unconditional love. No matter how bad the storm, we know with unwavering faith we all have the ability to stand in the center of that storm and trust it is there to shake out everything in our life that is no longer needed.

This is my lesson. Letting go of old ancestral beliefs has allowed me to stand back in my own personal power and my inherent wholeness. I first needed clarity on how I was showing up in the world. Then started to lean into those fears and rewire new beliefs. Finally, regulate my nervous system back to a level of safety. These modalities combined have allowed me to grow beyond my wildest dreams and now fully live my true life's purpose.

I would like to dedicate this chapter to my family, husband and my four beautiful children. Thank you for being my greatest teachers. I love you with all my heart.

Nineteen

The Journey to Myself

Moving from a Life of Shoulds to One of Purpose

MARIE SMITH

It started out as a whisper. *You can't keep this up.* This. What a loaded word. It meant so many things. Playing house. Saying yes to every volunteer job. Putting a smile on my face when I didn't feel like smiling.

At this point, my mother had been dead almost twenty years, but that didn't stop me from hearing her voice in my head telling me she loved me and was proud of me. The problem was I heard it loudest when I served others. I had somewhere along the line connected service and productivity with worthiness. Even though I worked part-time as a fitness instructor and personal trainer, I still thought of myself as a stay-at-home mom and put high value on it because that's what my mom was. I always wanted to be a mom when I grew up.

I felt like I needed to volunteer for every church and school job that fit in my schedule. If there was a need I thought I could fill, I filled it. It wasn't until years later that I adopted the philosophy of saying no so someone else could say yes. I looked outside myself for validation all the time. I was concerned with how things looked from the outside. Not so much my physical appearance, but more that I wanted to portray a happy family with no major problems.

I wasn't sad and wouldn't have described myself that way. I would have argued with you that I was happy because I had convinced myself I was. I do have an optimistic outlook on life, but my powerful mind might take it too far at times. You might call me delusional and unable to face reality. I would argue there's no reason to wallow in the misery, and we can make the best of any situation. The reality is probably somewhere in the middle.

I had a vision of what I thought my life "should" look like, and I wasn't at all tuned into what was actually going on. My husband felt ignored as I poured myself into our kids and community. While I made sure my kids didn't want for anything, I was ignorant of how much therapy could have helped them handle their big feelings or the tools that would have helped us all manage our emotions and behavior better. I give myself grace. I know I did the best I could with what I had at the time.

I can't remember exactly what it was that made me reach out for counseling help. My husband and I had gone to marriage counseling years earlier, which saved our marriage. Cheryl, our therapist, was the bridge that brought us back to each other. Now I needed an internal bridge to bring me back to myself.

I am the youngest of four kids. My closest sibling is six years older than me, and despite my mother's insistence that I was the only child who was planned, I imprinted with Primal Question number four, *Am I wanted?* (Foster, 2023). I always felt loved by my parents. My mom always told me she loved me and how special I was to her. My father had a harder time with emotions and as an adult, I know that was because of his childhood. As a child, I knew he loved me, he just showed in different ways. I do think I had a wonderful childhood. My siblings might say I was spoiled, but they were spoiled too because they got to experience my mother's healthiest years.

STOLEN MEMORIES

Mom was diagnosed with breast cancer when I was in the eighth grade. After surgery, high-dose chemotherapy, and two weeks of isolation in the hospital, she enjoyed about a year of remission before it came back. They treated it with radiation, but less than two years later, it had metastasized and she was never cancer free again.

From my junior year in high school until she died, my mother was in and out of chemotherapy, wore a chemo pump, participated in clinical trials, had some good days, and some bad ones. For a year, Dad drove her to Birmingham for an experimental treatment once a week. Her abdomen would fill with fluid and she would go to the hospital to have it drained. I remember her insisting I take her once when I was home from college. I think she knew of my tendencies to be blindly optimistic and wanted to prepare me for the future.

As the only child still living at home during most of her illness, I had to step up—or felt like I had to step up—to help take care of her. Thinking a little more of others and a little less of ourselves was practically the family motto. According to the Enneagram scale, I am a two, a Helper to my very core. One of the gifts of twos and Primal Question fours is that we are happy to do for others. We can anticipate needs and we fill them before you ask. Our downfall is we don't know when to stop. We often thrust our help on those who don't need or want it. When these folks reject that help, we see it as a full-on rejection of us. If we aren't needed by you, we must not be wanted at all, and therefore we have lost you and will fall into a tailspin.

My husband and I moved our wedding up from New Year's Eve to August 22, just three months after my college graduation and three months before his. The week of the wedding, Mom and I went to my final fitting, registered at two stores, got our nails done, and took care of all the last-minute wedding things. We dragged her oxygen tank with us and took our time, so she didn't get too out of breath along the way.

The morning of my bridesmaids luncheon, an ambulance came to the house at 3 a.m. to take her to the hospital for the last time. The next day, I put on my wedding gown in the room next to hers. The same gown that she, my aunt, and my sister had all worn on their wedding days. My dad walked me down the hospital hall turned wedding aisle into her room where John Henry and I were married at her bedside surrounded by our closest family and two friends. She died there three days later.

It was years later when I learned that on the day she was diagnosed, she told her best friend, "I have to see Marie get married." And she did! She saw to it that each of us was taken care of and she finally let go of the fight.

In her life before cancer and as much as she could after the diagnosis, Mom volunteered for everything. From the time I was four until she got sick, we kept about thirty foster babies. She was a room mother, drove on all the field trips, volunteered in the baby clothes closet at a local non-profit, and donated blood. When I was in high school, she and Dad were traveling during the regular Mother's Club meeting at my school. She started thinking back and realized she hadn't missed a meeting in twenty-six years. She was thoughtful and always bought little gifts that reminded her of someone. After she died, we found multiple boxes with names on them tucked away in her closet. Gift giving and acts of service were definitely her love languages.

The example I saw of a good mom was one who loved her kids and did all that she could for others. All I ever wanted was to be a mom and I followed her example, the good and the bad. Her temper was unpredictable and you never knew what was going to set her off, causing us to walk on eggshells sometimes. I found myself snapping at my kids like she used to do. I was irritated for no good reason and my reaction was often out of proportion to the situation. It was this realization coupled with the feeling I just wasn't doing anything well that spurred me to fill out my forms for individual counseling.

LEARNING TO SAY NO

Allison was my counselor's name and she had her work cut out for her. As someone who wants to serve others, it is hard to lay things out because I feel like I'm a burden. Yes, divulging these things to my therapist was hard, even though that is her job. I felt like I didn't want to put too much on her and what was I worried about anyway? I was fine; it would all be fine. It took a few sessions for me to open up and give her more than just the facts.

As a two, I feel others' feelings a lot. It is hard sometimes to know which ones are actually mine. That part was some work. I had spent so many years doing and feeling for others that I didn't know how to do or feel for myself. Self-care wasn't a thing for me. I certainly wasn't filling my own cup or putting my oxygen mask on first. I was doing and doing and giving and giving and didn't really know how to receive.

Allison helped me with that. She helped me figure out who I was, what I wanted, how I felt about things, and with the help of two best friends, introduced me to the concept of saying, "No."

I remember being on a call with two of my best friends and them asking why I was doing whatever the latest volunteer job was. This confused me greatly.

"Because they needed help."

"But why you?"

"...Um..."

They asked me if I really wanted to do it. I said, "I didn't mind helping out."

"No, do you **want** to do it?"

I had never thought about that before. I know that sounds crazy, but it is true. There was a need. I could fill it. So, I did. My desire had never entered my mind as something to consider. I was not the only mom in the school of seven hundred kids who might be available that day to volunteer. What they helped me see was by saying no, I was still being of service. My no allowed another person to say yes and have that experience. If I was always signing up first, I was keeping others from having a chance to get involved.

I started using two tools to help me decide when and where to help.

If it's not a hell yes!, then it is a hell no!

Wait one hour after the sign up goes out before clicking on it and signing up.

The first tool has helped me set boundaries and honor them, allowing me to live more authentically and in alignment with my core values. The second one freed me up to see new things. It allowed me to see where I really am needed and to not just jump on every opportunity. As I utilized these tools along with multiple self-care practices, I started to focus more on when and where I wanted to be of service.

In April of 2022, I was on a retreat prioritizing self-care, when I heard the call of the Holy Spirit in meditation. "You need to be a life coach," the voice said right in front of my nose.

Wait, what? I had never heard a voice before, and this one was calm and confident in this statement. I wasn't even sure what a life coach did!

I had been a personal trainer for a decade and toyed with exploring life coaching in the past, but the cost had always stopped me before I got too far in the research. Going into the retreat, I had thoughts of, *Is this all there is?* in regards to my career. And if this was it, was I okay with that? This voice along with a few other signs pushed me to look for a health and life coaching program. I found a dual certificate program and was able to finish it online in six months. In the midst of that, I started my own business and my next chapter began.

My life changed when I started tuning into my heart and following the call of the Holy Spirit. Door after door opened for me and things just worked out in a way they didn't before opening my heart and saying yes to God's call. I truly feel like I am living on purpose. I live for myself and not just for what I think my parents, family, or friends think I should do. Healing that emptiness in me I had filled by looking outward and doing for others has opened me up to be of service in a bigger way.

As a coach, I am extra aware of the butterfly effect that each of us creates. By helping clients and students, I start a wave of change that continues as they help others and those people help others, and it keeps going. That is true of each of us. Each and every one of us has the ability to change the world for the better. I am lucky I get feedback about how the tools I have taught have helped my students and their children and friends.

I often wonder how long the Holy Spirit was trying to get my attention, but I know I wasn't ready to hear it. I wouldn't have made a good life coach ten years ago. How could I have helped people be the best version of themselves when I didn't even know who I was? I took that journey back to myself, and I do the work to stay rooted there.

It starts with self-care and checking in with what is a true hell yes! It sounds simple, but if everything we do is like beating our heads against a wall, we can't possibly live on purpose. Each of us has a contribution to make to the world, a gift that no one else can give in the way that we can give it.

If you aren't sure if you are living on purpose, ask yourself, "Is this a hell yes?" with all that you do. You'll start getting some answers that point you in the right direction.

Twenty

Kintsugi: The Art of Resilience and Self-Love

How One Woman Triumphed Over Devastating Fatigue and Desperation

DR. KATHERINE ZHANG, PHD

In fifteenth-century Japan, under the soft glow of candlelight, the mighty military ruler Ashikaga Yoshimasa watched in dismay as his favorite tea bowl shattered into pieces out of his palms. Disheartened by the ugly metal staples used to mend such a delicate object, he sought a more aesthetic solution. Skilled Japanese craftsmen developed an ingenious method, blending lacquer with powdered gold to repair the cracks. When the bowl was returned, its shimmering golden veins transformed the shogun's sorrow into awe, unveiling a newfound beauty in its imperfections.

This masterful repair gave birth to Kintsugi, the traditional Japanese art of mending broken pottery with lacquer infused with powdered gold. Rooted in the philosophy of wabi-sabi, Kintsugi celebrates the history and resilience of objects, transforming their flaws into unique, visible features that tell a story of endurance and exquisiteness in imperfection.

Just as pottery is fragile, so too are our lives. We face chronic health battles, find ourselves trapped in unfulfilling careers, or struggle with financial hardship. Feeling flawed and broken, we often hide our imperfections, driven by society's relentless pursuit of perfection, showcased on social media. Kintsugi offers a sharp contrast to the perfectionism of modern society, teaching us to honor nobility in broken things.

By embracing our cracks and scars, we can find strength and beauty in our resilience, much like the art of Kintsugi. This philosophy is elegantly illustrated in the story of Cindy, a woman whose journey from overwhelming fatigue and despair to empowerment and renewal mirrors the essence of Kintsugi.

THE STORY

Cindy's life was once a smooth vessel, but over time, the pressures and strains of her existence caused it to crack. Her story is a testament to the transformative power of resilience, and how embracing our broken pieces can lead to a more profound and radiant existence.

It started as a whisper when she woke up one morning, *Get away, Cindy!* As days passed, the whisper grew louder, echoing in her mind no matter where she went.

One scorching August afternoon, Cindy was driving from work to pick up her kids from after-school. The stifling heat of the dog days of summer labored every breath. Sweat trickled down her neck, making her necklace itch, and her shirt clung to her damp skin. Her lower back throbbed with each press of the brake pedal, a sharp reminder of how long she'd been sitting in traffic.

"Gosh, I'm gonna be the last one to pick them up again," she muttered, thinking about her kids' disappointment. She pressed harder on the brake pedal, wincing. "Why is this stupid light still red?" she muttered. "Why am I going through this?"

Suddenly, the realization struck her like a brick. *Escape. What are you waiting for?* She blinked in disbelief, reading the two bumper stickers on the cars in front of her.

Cindy was a biologist working in a lab at a university. She was a mother of three: a ten-year-old and eight-year-old twins. She had suffered from chronic fatigue since her oldest was born. For ten years, she dreaded going to work and returned home even more exhausted from her stressful and demanding job.

Due to the torture of chronic fatigue and stressful life, she felt broken, unable to even look at herself in the mirror. For years, she had been proud of looking much younger than her age. People always thought she was in her early twenties. One day, while chatting, a neighbor lady inadvertently asked if she was in her forties. In reality, she was only thirty-nine. That casual remark pierced her heart so deeply. It was then she realized that no matter how hard she tried to hide her struggles, they were evident to others, etched onto her face. She hurried home and looked in the mirror. The bags under her eyes, the forehead wrinkles, and the nasolabial lines appeared like scars on her body and soul. Her once brilliant eyes had lost their sparkle and luster. She felt like a fallen porcelain piece, shattered and full of cracks.

Nonetheless, she kept neglecting the whisper until one day she got into a car accident. It wasn't her fault; the at-fault party was a young woman who begged her not to call the police, tears in her eyes. Out of empathy, Cindy didn't call. After all, it seemed like a minor accident—or so she thought.

The following week, Cindy attended a local conference. It involved a lot of walking between meeting rooms, and her left knee began to hurt. By the last day, walking had become very difficult, even with a knee brace. It turned out she had an acute contusion from the accident, worsened by all the walking. She decided to take a couple of days off to rest her knee but had technical problems submitting the request in the human resources portal over the weekend. She managed to email her boss on Monday morning and soon received approval for her leave.

She had no idea a bomb was about to drop.

A couple of hours later, she received an email from her boss, copied to two human resources personnel she didn't know. The email accused her of not submitting her weekly work outline the previous week and not submitting the leave request early enough. Cindy was confused, then enraged and humiliated. The weekly work outline wasn't even a formal requirement—many people in the lab hadn't been following it with no repercussions from the boss. The previous week, she had been at the conference and had nothing to update except conference materials, which she briefly reviewed with her boss at the lab meeting.

That was the last straw. *Enough is enough.* Cindy decided to resign. She still remembers the day of her resignation. The sky was clear and refreshing, wide, and bright. During her lunch break, she sat in the tranquil garden across the street. The fountain sang a gentle bubbling song, lilies emitted a light fragrance, and hummingbirds busied themselves collecting nectar.

After lunch, she handed in her resignation letter. As she left her boss's office, she felt a mix of relief, tinged with reckless bravery and stoicism. She had no idea where she was headed next, hadn't planned her next job, or figured out where the future income would come from. Yet, just like that, she left the place where she had poured her heart and soul for over a decade.

As she walked out of the laboratory building to the parking lot, she noticed an eagle soaring low overhead, circling her head as if conducting a ritual of renewal. She couldn't help but wonder if she had once been an eagle in a past life, longing to soar unrestricted through the sky.

"Nothing can stop my yearning for freedom," she hummed to herself, imagining a world where she could, "face the sea, with spring flowers blooming," as stated in a Chinese poem by Hai Zi.

Well, Cindy did not get a chance to face the sea, and flowers had not been blossoming in her world. She thought things would turn around now that she was not burdened with the stressful job. It didn't. She tried many things to cure her chronic fatigue—acupuncture, Traditional Chinese Medicine (TCM) herbs, supplements, chiropractic care—but nothing seemed to work. Some days, she felt better and optimistic, only to find herself relapsing into fatigue later, sometimes with even worse symptoms.

It felt as if a monster lived in her body, sucking out her energy from time to time. All the healing and treatments she tried only suppressed the monster but did not expel it, which was why it could still come out and haunt her, robbing her of strength and energy.

Her husband worked at a warehouse for minimum wage, their only income. His salary barely covered their expenses, forcing them to rely on savings and credit cards. The mounting credit card debts were nerve-wracking. Things would improve if she could reclaim the forty-thousand dollars a friend owed her, but he had moved out of state and cut contact.

You are so naïve to trust him. Why are you so stupid and gullible! she thought, hating herself.

"Honey, we can't afford that," became her mantra to the kids. "I hate inflation, Mommy."

"Mommy, why don't you find a job?" her oldest kid asked.

"Mommy wants to, but..." She didn't know how to complete the sentence, feeling pricked by a needle in her heart. *Who's gonna hire me? I literally have to lie in bed for hours every day*, she thought.

Another challenge Cindy experienced came from the complications of the car accident. After the accident, she began experiencing light sensitivity and blurry vision, which turned out to be post-concussion symptoms causing double vision. Despite the medical evidence, the insurance company refused to compensate her, exploiting her decision not to call the police at the scene.

One day, while lying down in bed coping with fatigue and headache, a figurine of a white ceramic angel on her bookshelf grabbed her attention. It was a beautiful figurine, pure and noble, with a white floor-length dress. However, it had lost its wings. Her twins had broken it accidentally.

What is the point of being an angel without wings? she thought. *What is the point of being a living human without energy?*

Why is all this happening to me? she wondered, feeling as if her life had become a cruel joke. She had always been the best student, attended the best university, and obtained the highest degree, only to end up a miserable, poor, and lifeless stay-at-home mom with no hope or future.

During the day, she kept up a facade for the kids, but at night, her emotional pain crept in. It felt like a heavyweight in her chest. In her mind, she visualized an old empty apartment with a loud crying baby girl inside. She could ignore it during the day, but at night, the baby girl's piercing cries were inescapable.

I wish I could cry for that little girl, but I can't, she thought, the years of bottling up emotions leaving her unable to shed tears. She imagined locking the crying child in a restroom, but the sound never stopped.

Desperate for an escape, one day she turned to online videos. A romance drama caught her eye. One episode turned into two, then three, and time slipped away—10 p.m., 11 p.m., 12 a.m., 1 a.m., 2 a.m. Days turned into nights, weeks into months, and before she knew it, watching romance dramas became her nightly ritual. *At least I don't have to think about my worries or pains,* she thought. Streaming videos became her painkiller.

The downside was waking up even more tired and foggy-brained, sometimes needing to go back to sleep the entire morning. Her energy levels became even worse and unpredictable, and she kept canceling schedules and pushing back to-do lists.

"You need to go to bed earlier," her doctor told her. "If you go to bed too late, it will damage your liver," said her acupuncturist. *Yes, I know. I just can't help it*, she thought. Watching videos was her chocolate, her smell of roses when roses weren't available.

When she did sleep, she had a recurring dream where she was diving down an endless abyss. She cannot fathom the meaning of this dream, but life indeed felt like an endless abyss to her. She needed help.

MENDING HER BROKEN WINGS

Despite being shackled by endless pain and hardship, Cindy's heart still yearned for light, hope, and renewal. One evening, Cindy decided to have a conversation with God. At one corner of her desk was a deck of cards, the *Tao Oracle* by artist Ma Deva Padma, featuring the sixty-four hexagrams of the *I Ching Book of Changes*.

She shuffled the deck carefully, whispered a prayer, held her breath, and drew a card. Turning it over, she saw the forty-eighth hexagram, The Well. She was amazed to see her abyss dream manifested in this card, as the illustration depicted a woman diving vertically into a bottomless well. The card spoke of "seeking truth," "wisdom," and "getting to the bottom of things." The explanation read, "The well is truth. Drinking from it takes time and patience and your full attention. To drink from the source of clarity within the depths of the self is to know the taste of Tao."

Encouraged, she drew two more cards: the eighteenth hexagram, Work on What Has Been Spoiled, and the sixty-second hexagram, Small Is Beautiful. The first card urged her to "heal," "make repairs," and "restore balance." It emphasized the importance of identifying unhealthy habits that contributed to her downward spiral. The second card advised her to "find the extraordinary in the ordinary", "slow down", and "learn to trust that life provides without you having to struggle to make it all happen".

Inspired by these insights, Cindy began to embrace her imperfections, recognizing her chronic fatigue as part of her unique story. She found solace in writing her stories and feelings, transforming pain into words that spoke of resilience. She also engaged in mindfulness practices like meditation, gentle yoga, and breath-work, reconnecting with her body as she tried to know the taste of Tao.

Amidst her other pursuits, she began learning to play the Guzheng, a Chinese plucked zither. The soothing melodies became her emotional outlet, allowing her to express the depth of her journey through music. As she strummed the strings, Cindy felt each note resonated with the understanding that every scar tells a story worth sharing.

She also decided to mend the broken angel figurine that had lost its wings, inspired by the art of Kintsugi. With meticulous care, she glued the wings back onto the angel using gold paint, creating shimmering lines that represented both the figurine's and her journey of healing.

Cindy sought support by joining a virtual group for spiritual practice, where she shared her story and found a connection with others who understood her struggles.

Instead of being trapped in the confines of her own problems, she decided to pursue a larger mission. Recognizing the profound impact of helping others, she trained as a coach, specializing in burnout prevention and resilience-building. She dedicated herself to empowering leaders and professionals to embrace their imperfections, fostering elevated well-being, and driving greater success.

Through her journey, Cindy discovered that Kintsugi was not merely about repairing broken objects but also about rebuilding one's spirit. She learned to accept and embrace her scars, understanding that they added substance and splendor to her life.

The angel figurine, with its golden veins, now stood as a symbol of her resilience and transformation. By embracing the art of Kintsugi, Cindy found a way to live authentically, uncovering strength in her vulnerabilities and grace in her imperfections.

Twenty One

Give Your Heart Wings

My Path From Healing to Harmony

JILL RAPPERPORT REISS

When I was thirty-five, I hit a wall of sheer exhaustion and serious, gnawing depression. I was a successful magazine publishing executive with a beautiful five-year-old daughter. I had just survived a bitter, wildly expensive, and brutal two-year divorce, which left me ragged. Each day, I had to muster all my energy to go to work, travel, attend meetings, make presentations, prepare proposals and reports, and care for my baby girl. It felt like I was moving through a sea of molten metal every day, with liquid lead running through my veins.

In the morning, my daughter would run into my bedroom, "Mama, wake up. Mama, wake up. Mama, wake up, let's play!"

Oh honey, Mama needs to sleep, I wanted to say. But looking at her beautiful face, I would drag myself out of bed, load up on coffee, and caffeine my way into the day.

I knew I was running on empty and couldn't sustain the life I was leading. I had a constant internal longing to do something that felt like it was coming from my heart and soul, making a contribution to the world while having a balanced life with my daughter. I felt trapped on the hamster wheel. I needed to support our household. I was making good money, but my heart was sinking, my body ached, and my stomach was always tight.

"Mama, let's go to the park," my daughter would say. *No time to enjoy the swings and the playground,* I thought.

"Buckle your seat-belt and hold on," I said to myself as I was catapulted into a day filled with back-to-back meetings and nary a second to breathe.

One day, I had a meeting with a beautiful woman who seemed to float on air as she glided across the floor. We sat down, and after introductory comments, I abandoned my sales agenda and asked, "May I ask you, what is your beauty secret?"

"Do you really want to know?" she replied.

I nodded.

"I have a guru." She paused, searching my face, her eyes glued to mine. "A guru is a great master, a self-realized being. She has given me a mantra."

"Please tell me more about this," I said.

"A mantra is a sacred sound; it is the energy of the Divine in sound form." As she spoke, I felt my body respond, softening and quickening at the same time.

Then she said the words of the mantra, "Om Namah Shivaya." My hair stood on end, and I got goosebumps.

"Please repeat that," I said.

"Om Namah Shivaya.".

I tried to say it, stumbling over the words. "Please write it for me," I asked.

As she did, she told me about the meditation center she attends, "You can go there anytime; if you want, I'll meet you there."

I went home and put that piece of paper under my pillow for weeks, saying the mantra over and over again, feeling deep peace. One evening, I drove by the meditation center and saw people gathering in the front courtyard. I went in, was met by warm, friendly people, got an introduction to their practices, and went into the meditation hall. When the chanting began, I felt a peace come over me, and after a short while, tears streamed down my cheeks. I discovered the heart-opening practice of chanting and meditation. I joined a regular yoga practice. I shared what I learned with my daughter, her friends, and the Girl Scout troop that a fellow professional mom and I had formed when our girls were in kindergarten.

For me, Spirit speaks through all events and circumstances, and like waves in the ocean, her messages keep coming until I listen and muster the courage to act.

On September 11, 2001, I was in Hawaii, participating in Tony Robbins' Life Mastery program. What I witnessed convinced me that it was possible for miracles to occur. There were two thousand people there from all over the world.

Tony invited onto the stage with him a radical Pakistani and an extremist Israeli man who were screaming words of hatred toward one another, inflamed by the attack on the U.S. Through a process of conflict resolution (shifting into different states of being and consciousness), they simultaneously experienced such a shift in perspective that they ran across the stage, embracing each other as loving brothers! There wasn't a dry eye in the auditorium. Later, it was documented on *Larry King Live*. In this pivotal moment, I made the decision that I wanted to be a part of this much-needed shift in consciousness.

I am an angel of transformation who nurtures souls, lights the way, and creates peace and abundance. This emerged as a soul mission for me, and I have lived my life out of it ever since. The fast-paced publishing workplace was not the place to have this conversation. My daughter really needed me. I was living my life as if there were a million tomorrows. I realized that the conflict between my current life and what I really felt called to do was causing me physical, mental, and spiritual pain.

Three more events in quick succession caused me to take massive action on my soul dream. I was the group publisher of a group of Spanish-language pan-regional business magazines, working tirelessly from morning till the wee hours of the night. We had a global sales staff, and everyone needed assistance, answers, support, and management to meet our aggressive revenue goals.

In preparation for a business trip to Mexico, I took my car to the dealership. The service manager shared with me a picture of a beautiful young boy, six years old. He was the son of very good friends, and the service guy was in grief because the boy had just passed away.

"The boy got a rare form of brain cancer; the family flew him everywhere to try to save him, and he just passed away," he cried.

It hit me in the back of my heart and felt like a direct message from Spirit. *What am I doing with my life and my daughter?*

The next day in Mexico City, while on a short break from meetings, my cellphone rang. It was my daughter's school.

"Hi Jill, can you come and get your daughter?"

"No, I'm in Mexico. What's happening?"

"There has been an internet incident, and she is crying hysterically." My heart skipped a beat.

"Can I speak with her?"

"No, she's in with the school nurse."

"I am in Mexico City, oh dear." Her father was on business in Brazil, and my parents, who live in Miami, were also out of town. "Ok, I'll call Mary, our nanny, to pick her up." My heart ached. *What is this internet incident?*

Mary went to get my daughter, and I continued back into the meeting room around the big conference table. Somehow, we got the contract signed, and I left for the airport.

I was sitting at the gate waiting to board my flight. The Mexico City airport was a lively place in those years. There were mariachi bands floating around, lots of fun Latin music piping in, and festive foods and drinks available at every turn. I sat listening to some of my favorite songs, "Guantanamera" and "De Colores," playing.

Surprisingly, an American song began to play. I could hardly believe it, the song by Harry Chapin "Cats in the Cradle." The ballad of a father not having enough time to spend with his son, and the son growing up to be just like his father. Ok, Spirit, I hear you! This is the last straw! I'm taking charge. My life isn't going to be that song!

I heard my flight called for boarding and got in line.

When I arrived back home, I vowed to myself to say something, to do something. So I mustered up my courage, created a proposal for flexible hours, less travel, and providing leadership and developing others to take on some of my work. I met the next day with the CEO and made my proposal.

The CEO said, "You see Kathleen there? She has two children, and she works until two a.m. here in the office. And you see Manuel? He has a wife and kids, and he travels and works hard too. I can't make that arrangement for you."

From deep within my being, I remember so clearly, this voice came out, as if I had no control over it, and what I said was a surprise to myself, "Ok, then I am giving you one month's notice starting now. I am resigning."

My fearful naysayer voice was screaming, *What are you going to do? What are you saying? You have stock options and partial ownership and a great salary. How are you going to survive?*

But the voice that spoke was firm and sure. I went home, stunned and excited. I told my daughter I would be home with her more from now on.

Now what do I do?

With the help of my wisdom community, a really great coach, friends, and my parents, I made a plan to downsize, not knowing what I would do. I sold my big house; our nanny retired; I sold my gold Volvo; and gave away all my business suits; and we packed up and moved to a smaller house. My father helped me get a Honda, and I began the process of detoxing and de-stressing.

I had already been studying and practicing NLP (Neuro Linguistic Programming) and NAC (Neuro-Associative Conditioning). I was working with sound healing, chanting and meditation, and yoga. These trainings and practices contributed to resolving the depression and the exhaustion.

When I told my Girl Scouts I had resigned and didn't know what I was going to do, one of them raised her hand and said, "Ms. Jill, we love when you teach us yoga. Why don't you teach yoga?"

I said, "Well, I teach you what I do, and your parents know me, but I'm not certified to teach."

And then she said the obvious, which until that moment wasn't obvious to me, "But Ms. Jill, can't you get certified?"

The next week, I was enrolled in my first yoga teacher training and began my post-corporate life. My body, mind, and spirit aligned. Yoga teacher training and dedicated practice was like a fountain of youth! I had never felt so good in my body. I became a vegetarian, and my arthritis and severe body pain went away. My face softened. People said I lost ten years.

I created a yoga school and certification training for children, teachers, and parents, teaching over ten-thousand hours to children from ages two to eighteen. A voracious thirst for all things wellness, nutrition, meditation, metaphysics, meta-psychology, energy healing, indigenous and shamanic practices, soul retrieval, indigenous ceremonies, trauma resolution, quantum physics, neuroscience, Akashic records reading and women's cycle awareness and healing led me to my new life.

Since then, I have never looked back. I am now known as the Urban Shaman, helping hundreds of people heal from traumas, move their lives in fulfilling and healthy directions, shift out of old identities into new ones, and find authentic alignment in their lives. For the past twenty-two years, I have witnessed hundreds of amazing healing experiences in my private spiritual coaching and healing sessions, workshops, and retreats, and in my Shamanic sound bowl meditations that I offer.

If you are longing to heal and make a shift in your life, find people to support you and have faith. Hire a coach, a spiritual guide, surround yourself with people who help you believe you can do this and survive. When fears come up, find someone to support you as you move beyond that fear.

"Let go of your ego!" I had to go through a huge readjustment because I was a bigwig, and I had to transform how I measured success.

I've found that connecting with Spirit begins with viewing my life events from a high vantage point. I start by taking long, slow, and deep breaths, which helps me detach and see my life from a new perspective. I imagine myself standing on a mountain peak, looking down at the path I've traveled. From this elevated view, I reflect on what I see and sense. Once I've connected with this perspective, I take a moment to journal my thoughts, focusing on the values and beliefs that emerge from this experience.

Grounding with nature is another powerful practice. Whether I choose to sit, stand, or lie down on the earth, I feel a deep connection with the grass, trees, and soil beneath me. As I breathe deeply, I allow nature to reset my nervous system, clearing the energy field of my body. This practice helps me relieve physical ailments and brings a sense of calm to my emotional and mental states.

Finally, I find healing sounds to be a path to harmony. I seek out a quiet place to rest and listen to the soothing tones of crystal bowls or other sacred instruments. These sounds harmonize my energy field, activating both my higher mind and heart.

We are in the time of the Pachakuti, the turning of ages, a new dawning era. This ancient Andean Shaman prophecy speaks about these times now. It is a turning of values and principles to the feminine energetic principles of love, sacred balance, honoring all of life, and mother earth as one whole being. This will be achieved when we know we are part of an interconnected whole, none of us is separate. Spirit calls us to be full heart and soul and give lovingly to ourselves and others. Take a leap and be a part of that turning.

Twenty Two

Blazing a New Path

A Journey of Healing, Self-Discovery, and Empowerment

CATTERINA CALDERON

I t was a beautiful morning in North Carolina when I settled into my office to make a couple of work calls. Glancing at my phone, I noticed a missed call from the hospital. Having undergone minor surgery the week before, I thought, *How thoughtful. They are calling to check on me.*

As I completed my first work call, I noticed another missed call from the hospital. This time, my doctor left a voicemail.

I can't believe she is calling to see how I am feeling. I loved the hospitality in North Carolina as I had just moved there. I called back and as I was going to leave a voicemail, she answered.

"Thank you so much for calling, I am doing really well," I said.

"That's not why I'm calling," she replied. "I'm calling because we just got the results from the pathologist."

Silence.

My mind raced as soon as she mentioned the pathologist. *Pathologist?*

Then she threw me a curve-ball. "They found a tumor, and we need to discuss your options."

Options? Why do I need options? Before I could fully process it, the words came out, "Are you saying I have cancer?"

"There's a chance I removed everything, but we need to schedule an appointment with an oncologist."

Again, my mind raced as I was processing the information. *Oncologist? Tumor? Shit, I should have paid more attention in biology class.*

"I've already set up an appointment, but you're free to choose another doctor if you prefer," she continued.

"When is it?"

"Tomorrow if you can make it," she replied.

I noted the details and immediately called my dad. "Papá, I thought you said the doctor mentioned that everything went well."

Silence on the other end.

"That's what the doctor said. Why?" my dad asked.

"The doctor just called and told me they found a tumor." His voice shifted with concern, "What are the next steps?"

As I explained, I could sense his worry growing. "Papá, please don't tell anyone yet. I don't want people talking about me as if I already have cancer," I said, mindful of the energy I wanted to attract. He understood and reassured me, "Go to your appointment, and we'll talk afterward."

That's what I loved about my dad; he was always practical and direct. From a young age, he taught me to go with the flow.

One day on the beach, a wave caught me. As I surfaced, the first person I saw was my dad.

"Are you okay?" he asked. I stood up, feeling scared and on the verge of tears. "Did you feel the current take you?" he asked.

I nodded.

"Water up your nose?"

I nodded.

"Next time, go with the current instead of fighting it," he advised, extending his arm for me to grab. I took hold, and together we swam back to the shore.

That day stayed with me. Instead of instilling fear of the ocean, my dad taught me to respect the current and work with it rather than struggle against it. I've carried that lesson into other areas of my life. Sometimes, we find ourselves caught in challenging situations, but if we go with the flow, we can navigate through them and enjoy the present moments. This time was no different.

The day of the appointment with the oncologist arrived. That morning, I dressed up, even wore my favorite high heels wanting the doctor to see me and not a sick patient. After finishing my hair, I looked at myself in the mirror and said, "You are not sick."

Arriving at the parking lot, I asked the attendant if this was the right place. "Looking for the cancer center?" he inquired.

I nodded.

"Are you the patient?" he continued. I felt a jolt, a knot formed in my throat, and I hesitated.

"No," I began to say. "I have an appointment with an oncologist." I paused, then realized, "I guess...Yes, I am the patient."

As I walked through the hospital, I noticed the signs in the hallways with the word 'cancer' on them. It was hard to believe that I could be the patient, given that I was young, ran half marathons, and maintained healthy eating habits.

I gave my name to the receptionist. She looked up with a puzzled expression and asked in an almost disbelieving tone, "Are you the patient?" This time, I replied with confidence, "It seems so."

When the nurse called my name, I stood up. She glanced at me and then at my file. "Didn't you have surgery last week?" she asked.

"Yes."

"Should you be wearing those heels?"

I smiled. "I'm walking slow."

She chuckled and said, "Girl, you're going to be just fine." That's exactly what I wanted—to be seen for who I am, not as a sick patient.

As I waited for the doctor, a nurse came to collect my chart. When the doctor walked in without it, I found it odd. How would she know about my case? As she sat down, I sensed something was wrong, but being unfamiliar with this type of situation, I waited.

She began by asking about symptoms, some of which I realized I had overlooked. Then came another curve-ball.

"We need you to undergo another procedure; there's a possibility that the cancer could be spread."

In shock I replied, "My gynecologist didn't mention this."

"I just spoke with the pathologist. We need to rule it out."

"When should I schedule this?" I asked, feeling my anxiety rise.

"My team is arranging it now, which is why they took your chart. You should have it this week. Any other questions?"

"Yes, if it has spread, what might the prognosis be in terms of years?"

She regarded me with compassion. "If it has spread, it could be anywhere from five to ten years or more, but we don't know for sure yet. Our priority is to gather all the facts. After that, we'll discuss the best course of action together."

As I walked towards my car, the words "five to ten years" echoed in my mind. Should I cry? Why am I not crying? In movies, the character would be in tears.

Then I locked eyes with someone in the hallway, and she offered me a warm smile. She didn't know, but that smile meant the world to me. Inspired by her kindness, I decided to smile at everyone I passed on my way to the car. I wondered if they, too, were experiencing similar challenges and uncertainty. If so, I hoped my smile conveyed the same warmth and hope I had just felt.

As the automatic door opened to the outside, I looked up at the sky and said, "It's a beautiful day." Standing there, I took it all in, admiring the beauty and calmness it brought me. I didn't want to take that beautiful day for granted.

Then I turned on the car, and one of my favorite songs played. Reflecting on my life, I said to myself, "I've had a good life. Thank you, God."

Afterward, I called my dad, who encouraged me not to jump to conclusions and to wait for the results.

I underwent the procedure and soon after, I received the call that there was no cancer elsewhere, but we needed to discuss next steps, including the potential side effects of chemotherapy.

During my follow-up meeting with the doctor, we went over my options, including the possibility of a hysterectomy. When the doctor brought it up, I choked up, realizing it meant I would never have children. Since my divorce, I had told myself that although I love kids, I would be okay if motherhood didn't happen for me. But in that moment, the reality struck hard: This decision would mean giving up on motherhood.

My mind raced with questions: Will the treatment be painful? How many sessions will there be? Will I lose my hair? Will I be able to work? Will my insurance cover this? Will I need help?

Then I heard the doctor say I would experience fatigue.

"You will likely lose energy, experience muscle pain, become weaker."

When she said "weaker," something inside me reacted, and I interrupted her, "No, I am strong. My body might become weaker, but my mind will remain strong."

For some reason, the term "weaker" unsettled me. I couldn't envision myself as weak.

After considering all the options, I agreed to proceed with chemotherapy. It was a lot to process, especially since I didn't know many people or have my family or friends close by.

After the doctor's appointment, I went to lunch with my friend who had accompanied me. As we reviewed the paperwork, she mentioned that some people don't lose their hair. While I appreciated her attempt to comfort me, I knew I had to face the reality that I likely would. Seeing the concern in her eyes made me realize how this was impacting not just me but also my loved ones. We took a photo before she returned to New York, which I keep as a reminder of the day my life changed and the start of a new chapter marked by uncertainty and resilience.

The day of my first chemo session arrived. Entering the room with my mom, I saw other patients and made eye contact with one who smiled at me, easing my nerves. As the medications started, I felt strange.

Glancing at the patient next to me, I said, "I don't like this."

She smiled. "Feels weird?"

I nodded.

"Don't fight it, let yourself go." From that moment on, her words got me through every treatment.

Shortly after my first treatment, while walking my dog, Brutus, I felt the wind in my hair. When I ran my fingers through it, a large chunk came out in my hand. I thought to myself, *This is it. The nurse warned me that my hair would start falling out. I continued walking, letting it fall.*

Back home, I shaved off the remaining hair. It felt strange to see myself in the mirror. As I began to adjust to this new version of myself, I made a promise. Looking into the mirror, I met my own eyes and said, "Your hair doesn't define you; I love you."

From that morning onward, it became a ritual to wake up, look myself in the eye, and say, "I love you."

Later, I went to my mom's room, where she was staying to help me out during my chemotherapy treatment. I said, "Mamá, the hair is gone."

She woke up quickly and found her glasses. Then she looked up at me, tears welling in her eyes.

"Mamá, you should be happy," I reassured her. "It means the chemo is working. We should be grateful."

My mom is strong, but seeing the pain in her eyes was heartbreaking. I knew she felt helpless, but she had already given me what I needed: belief, trust in God and perseverance. She taught me never to give up once committed. I started chemo, I was determined to see it through.

One day, I decided to stop wearing scarves on my head. As I ran an errand with my mom, she said, "Why don't you wear your scarf?"

"I prefer to go bald, why? Not a good look?" I replied with playful sarcasm.

She hesitated. "No, I just don't like how people stare at you."

"Mamá, who cares if they stare? I'm getting healthier," I said trying to lift her spirits. She grinned.

As I reflect on this, I realized I had learned to reframe how I saw myself. I didn't see a bald person; I saw someone getting healthier. Given a chance to live, I wondered why and what my life would look like after the treatments.

A few months after finishing chemotherapy, my dad was diagnosed with stage four cancer and passed away shortly after. I struggled to understand why I was given a chance to live while he was not. He had a family—grandkids, children, and a wife—while I had only Brutus. My dad fought even harder than I did, yet here I was, still alive, and he was gone.

I wondered if he endured the same uncertainty, fears, pain, and symptoms that I had. Did he wrestle with the same questions about life's purpose? Did he feel fulfilled? How I wished I could call him and ask—I'm sure he would have had a practical answer, like he always did. Now he was gone, and the question kept coming up: What was the purpose? As I worked through these emotions, I knew I had been given an opportunity to live, and I wanted my life to mean something.

A NEW CHAPTER

I had a successful career in top organizations and held high-level positions, but I still felt a sense of emptiness. When I became ill, it became clear that my body was trying to communicate with me. I realized I had been driven by external expectations and ego, rather than by a sense of purpose.

During this time, I focused on finding my purpose and explored coaching, Neuro-Linguistic Programming (NLP) and hypnosis. Drawn to these modalities for their ability to harness the mind's power, promote subconscious healing, and reshape reality, I discovered how inner healing and intuition can impact our lives, especially during illness.

One valuable tool I learned was reframing situations—a technique I instinctively used throughout my journey. Reframing involves identifying a challenge, such as my cancer diagnosis, and acknowledging the accompanying fear and uncertainty. By examining my thoughts and beliefs, questioning negative assumptions, and seeking a positive perspective, I could shift my mindset.

Visualizing myself overcoming the challenge made the goal feel more attainable. I created an action plan with manageable steps, like attending treatments and maintaining a healthy diet. Integrating these steps into my daily routine helped reinforce a positive mindset and taught me that while I couldn't control every aspect of my situation, I could control my response.

Another technique I used was positive self-talk in a mirror, which I later discovered was taught by Louise Hay. This practice became a powerful tool for building resilience, facing fears with courage, and deepening my connection with myself. By intentionally facing our wounds, we gain wisdom that aids our healing and empowers us to inspire others.

I now believe that finding one's purpose is a journey of self-discovery and growth. Approach each day with intention, stay open to life's offerings, and listen to your intuition. Embracing this mindset led me to become a coach and facilitate programs that help others find clarity and purpose through life transitions, while also staying open to new experiences and insights that shape my own path.

Now, every smile I receive reminds me of the strength and resilience within us all. Never underestimate how powerful a smile can be. Share your smile—Say cheese!

Twenty Three

Journey of a Joy Rebel

Facing the Shadows to Find the Light

MARIA BRANNON

In the stillness of Mom's house, I opened the front door to collect a package from the porch as a blur of feathers darted inside, sparrow's wings beating a frantic rhythm against the air. Leo, my mom's enormous Maine Coon cat, sprang from his perch across the room, a streak of gray and white fur, eyes wide in hot pursuit. I just arrived in Little Rock from Nashville to stay and take care of Leo while Mom was in the hospital. Once the excitement subsided, I escorted our feathered friend to the open garage, wished it goodnight, put my groceries away, and turned my attention back to Leo, who was still amped up.

I wandered slowly through rooms filled with intentional vignettes of beautiful art, family photos, and tiny treasures collected over the years. My chest tightened a little as I recalled the legal papers my sister and I signed years ago, their significance now looming over me. The thought of digging through her organized chaos felt daunting but necessary.

I searched the kitchen desk, the makeshift work area in her dining room, then made my way into her bedroom and approached the giant carved wooden wardrobe.

Could this please be a portal to Narnia?

Instead, I found another kind of portal made of multicolor file folders filled with memories spanning at least four decades. Family trips, old divorce agreements from when she and my dad split up in the eighties, art accolades, articles, and awards from her long career as a fine artist.

How did I forget what a badass my mom is?

A few folders labeled "San Miguel de Allende" called out to me, and curiosity had me scooping the folders out of the wardrobe and onto my mom's bed before I thought twice. Receipts from shops we'd visited, restaurants, the house we rented, and the face of an innocent summer crush.

How many decades ago was that? I was only thirteen.

Details fade like an old dream, but from what I recall, San Miguel de Allende was a vibrant tapestry of colorful flowers, intricate art, stunning architecture, and charming cobblestone streets. We were there for a three-week adventure with several of my mom's artist friends. I was to take immersive Spanish classes and soak up the culture during the summer between seventh and eighth grade.

Long known as a popular destination for expats and folks with second homes, there was no shortage of other American teens. A group of us made fast friends and roamed around town together while our parents did whatever they were doing.

One night my new friends and I got permission to go to the disco, and the cute local boy who flirted with me all week was there. Language barriers dissolved as we swayed together on the dance floor. Tangy orange juice mingled on my tongue with his salty kisses as the club got more crowded. The room started spinning. *Maybe it's just the heat.*

I was feeling disoriented and confused as he offered to help me outside for some air. *Wait, where is he leading me?*

I lost consciousness after my back slammed down against the cold metal floor of an empty cargo van. I vaguely remember other men seeing this happen, laughing, and doing nothing.

Where am I?

I woke up in a quaint hospital room, mom by my side. One of the other American boys from our group found me laid out on one of those beautiful cobblestone streets, losing a lot of blood. He and his dad got me to safety and contacted my mom. I wish I could thank that angel from Montgomery—that's all I remember about him. As a thirteen-year-old, I certainly didn't know how to process any of what just happened, and I blamed myself. I tried to rush the process of forgiveness, both toward him and the whole traumatic event.

Maybe the pain of this will fade as quickly as the bruises on my body had started to.

Back then, I was very connected to God from a Christian lens. I'd grown up going to a Methodist church and an evangelical Christian summer camp for years. So, when this happened, I thought, *I'm lucky this wasn't any worse.*

Some part of me knew it wasn't my fault, but my faith led me to believe it was my duty to forgive him and the whole situation without acknowledging any of the helplessness, shame, rage, or confusion I felt. I built a mental wall to keep the trauma at bay, believing it would protect me.

Mom did her best to support me when we returned, and the school year started. She scheduled my follow up appointments and found a therapist for me. I only know this because I've been *told* that's what happened; I have no personal memory of going to that therapist. Apparently, I had six sessions with her.

I recall my dad's well-intentioned advice, "The sooner you can get over it, the better."

I wanted to be a good girl and move on with my life, so I did such a good job of forgetting that I also managed to forget most of the details of my junior high and high school years. During that time, a fragment of my soul panicked and flew out of my body just like that little sparrow on Mom's door; it wasn't safe to be there and feel all the feelings. As an adult, I've healed over the decades to tear down that wall, reclaim my power, and be fully present in my body. Singing and using my voice has been a huge part of that process.

Back in my mom's bedroom with papers and memories strewn around me, I noticed the anniversary date of my hospital stay in Mexico was coming up in a few days. For decades we both carried heavy baggage from that long-ago trip, packed with guilt and subconscious anger. With wisdom's vantage, I understood how it shaped our challenging relationship. I treasured how much we softened and grew in our depth of love for each other over the last ten years.

I don't believe in coincidences. I am here now, whole, and healed to stay by my mom's side while she's in the hospital. Now it's my turn to hold her hand through the scary stuff.

My beautiful artistic mom with all her talent and magnetic intensity had long battled with bouts of deep depression. She was only diagnosed with bipolar disorder later in her life, and I wondered if she was someone who could be labeled the modern term of Highly Sensitive Person. Someone who feels things so deeply it takes all their energy just to maintain some semblance of normalcy before needing to unplug and retreat from it all. Someone who had her own deep traumas that caused her tender soul fragments to fly away to protect what was left.

What if that's what made it so hard for her to stay balanced and present?

In more recent years, I learned about Human Design and that my mom had the energetic blueprint of a Projector *(highly sensitive to the people and environments they are in, needing much time alone)*. This revelation made sense to me. Of course she would need to withdraw to recharge, and it gave me a lot more empathy for things that used to drive me bonkers about her.

I'm so grateful to be of service to her now, the past doesn't matter.

On my way across town to the hospital I see several square-headed, brown-gray feathered, majestic Cooper's hawks circling overhead, a silent reminder to keep a higher perspective of whatever we may face as a family.

Mom's eyes lit up as she saw me arrive at the Intensive Care Unit. "Perfect timing" the nurses said. "Your mom's being moved to a regular room."

Relieved I think, *Great, we can get this figured out and plan the next steps.*

The stars strangely aligned so I'd be the sole in-person caretaker and advocate for Mom over the coming weeks. I helped her get settled in the new room and got to know the shift nurses. Mom's voice was in my head reminding me to, *Take notes when a loved one is in the hospital. You must advocate for them and make sure details aren't missed since staff are always stretched thin and in a hurry. Will do, mom, I've got you.*

On day three, I decided to wear one of my favorite T-shirts when I visited. She noticed it right away and asked, "What's a joy rebel, and what does the lightning bolt mean between the words?"

I told her about a Wonder Workshop that my husband and I attended years ago that was hosted by Kid President creator, Brad Montague, and one of his messages was to be a Joy Rebel and choose joy, especially in the hard times.

Mom and I had a lovely conversation about what it means to have that powerful choice in the face of the challenges that life inevitably presents us with. When I shared that conversation with my husband later, he sent me a picture of the back of an unframed painting he'd rediscovered that Mom had given me years ago. In her handwriting it said, "For Maria, my inspiration of Joy!"

A couple of weeks later, we're at a hospital rehab facility with a solid plan of building her strength back up. She's alarmingly frail.

It breaks my heart to see her struggle to speak, feed herself, sit up, or even hold her phone. My mind was spinning as I realized *life may look very different moving forward. I'm not sure she'll be able to be on her own for at least a few months while she recovers some mobility. After that, who knows?*

Between visits, I found myself noticing her keepsakes with fresh eyes, each item a window into her rich, complex life. Something hanging in her art studio caught my attention, *I must take this to her.*

When I was little and she struggled with depression, I made her a small portable rainbow out of polymer clay. Its muted colors are subtle with a convenient carrying handle, like a little handbag. She'd kept it all these decades. *This situation calls for a portable rainbow.*

When I was younger, I declared to my family around age four or five that I wanted to be called Rainbow M, so rainbows were always kind of a thing between us, for multiple reasons.

We made it through another week, so I finally took a break by going for a massage that my sister and her husband gifted me. Back in my car afterwards feeling so relaxed, *I really needed that; kind of hate to check my phone now, but I'd better.*

Notifications of messages and voicemails cascade on the screen. The nurse said, "Your mom's being transported back to the ICU via ambulance, and you should meet her at the emergency room now."

Any sense of relaxation quickly drained from my body. I called my sister and headed to the ER to wait for Mom's arrival. We got situated in a temporary room and nurses said they'd, "run some tests and get IVs going with fluids and a unit of blood, her sodium is dangerously low, and iron levels, too."

Hours passed until she's moved back up to an ICU room, a strangely familiar place now, the nurses tell me, "She's stable, you should go home to get some rest."

At this point, it's after visiting hours and I'd discovered that the hospital had the most incredible giant cement stairwells with cathedral-like acoustics any singer would die for. *Singing is a release and makes me feel better, so I'll slip into the stairwell for a secret song offering my prayers for mom.*

Walking down the stairs, each otherworldly sound swirled around me as my voice flowed along with my tears. "Songbird" by Christine McVie came to mind, and I let the lyrics penetrate my heart with more depth than ever before.

During the third week, she's in ICU for two nights, then moved to a regular room. On that sunny Tuesday morning I left her house to go sit with her and noticed an iridescent shimmer of light on my windshield. The most perfect single dragonfly wing was magically tethered there, a symbol of transformation that mom has long resonated with. I marveled at its colors and patterns, delicate yet strong. I wondered, *Is my mom starting her transition?*

Later, at mom's bedside, one of her closest friends texted and asked me to read mom a short poem she sent—it was about a dragonfly. Out of the blue that evening, a friend of mine in Nashville sent me a story about the dragonfly. Signs and confirmations all around, *she's making ready to transmute her current form.*

I ask mom if she's scared and she says, "Only for how long it might take before it's over."

A biopsy finally revealed an aggressive and widespread cancer. The next several days I facilitated short visits for dear longtime friends and family members to sit with her and give their love. My dad stopped by, and I could see in his glistening eyes, he knew what I did. I told my sister they needed to expedite their return travel plans and they made it back on Saturday. We were all with her as much as possible before she died peacefully, surrounded by love the following Tuesday.

The quickness of her passing was a shock to us all but a merciful release for her. She unfurled her spirit wings, leaving behind the burdens that had weighed her down.

A week later, as my husband and I made our way back to Nashville, we kept getting detours, even our detours had detours. What should've been a five-hour drive took over seven.

I'm beyond ready to be back home, but I surrender to the timing of this journey. I told myself, *The path forward isn't always straightforward, and we'll get there eventually.*

At our neighborhood's freeway exit, a huge rainbow stretched out directly in front of us. Most of the sky was sunny except for one golden curtain of rain. Following us back to our house, the rainbow curved over our rooftop. *I've got to see this from our backyard*, so I hurried through the house. *The rainbow is still shining bright.*

Moments later I called for my husband to come out. "Look, it's a double rainbow now!" It stayed like that for over thirty minutes! I received that as a sign from my artistic mom, painting the sky in beauty. Yes, Mom, *I choose to be a joy rebel and will always look for the rainbows.*

Twenty Four

All the Seasons Lead Back Home

A Journey from Depression to Embodiment

MASHA VENTA

I t was a beautiful spring day, I was running around with my friends in the safe, beautiful, medieval city of Ljubljana. My school was located five minutes away from my house. All my friends lived five minutes away from school. Every day was the same yet just a little different.

Spring is the best season. Flowers bloom, birds sing, the sun shines. Grass is green. It's so safe, and seven-year-old children walk home from school by themselves.

We were a happy family. There were dysfunctions, but I just wasn't aware of them. The good vastly outnumbered the bad. At that point in my life, self-doubt was not in my vocabulary. I was happy with the world, happy with others, happy with myself. Thoughts like, *I'm not good enough* or *I need to make myself smaller to fit it* never even crossed my mind.

I had my mom, my dad, my grandma, my friends, my neighborhood, my school.

I performed with confidence at school functions, singing at the top of my voice, dancing freely. I spent every single free moment at friends' houses, at activities, in parks, traveling, walking home with my grandma who would entertain me by recounting "The Hound of Baskerville".

I thought life would always be like this, moving at the speed of honey.

FALL

When the leaves started falling, so did my life.

My parents got a divorce. It wasn't sudden, there were definitely disagreements, but you never plan for something like that. My mom and I had to move out and move into a house in the countryside, miles away from my friends and everything that was familiar.

My parents were not in the happiest of marriages and I felt it. I rationalized that it was better if they called it quits. It is better for me, for them, for everyone.

However, I never went through a proper grieving process. With nowhere to go, all of that anger, confusion, and hurt turned inward. The fear, darkness, sadness, and abandonment were numbed with television. Hours upon hours of shows and movies. Not because I wanted to watch them, but because I wanted to escape. An addiction to the screen was born. A reprise for my brain. A way to shut off and shut down.

My mom dealt with my depression by sending me to boarding school, then brought me back, sent me away, and brought me back again. Instead of emotional support and understanding, I got exiled. Not that I can blame anyone—culturally we weren't taught how to handle big emotions.

At fourteen, I changed schools for the fourth time. At this point, I lost interest in school, friends, and life. I fell into a deep, dark, bleak depression. I had no one there for me to just check in on how I was processing it all. Processing the loss of family. The process of losing my childhood home. The process of losing my friends.

I started believing that if this horrible thing happened to me, it *must* be my fault, right? So thoughts that were never there in childhood, started announcing themselves over the PA in my head daily. *You're not good enough. Everyone hates you. You're failing. Never show your true self to others because they will reject you.*

Besides numbing, I started controlling myself. I turned all this anger and aggression inward. I thought, *If I can just control every thought, control the way people perceive me, control what happens to me, then I will never have to feel pain again and everything will be alright.*

But that's not how life works, right? There's no way to hide and suppress your life force because it **will** find a way to come out, whether you like it or not.

For some, that happens through disease. For me, it happened through an unwillingness to live. A tightness in my chest. A constant anxiety. An inability to express myself and connect with people. A deep-seated feeling that something was not quite right and there was so much more to life.

Fall in Ljubljana crushes your soul. The capital is tucked between a circle of mountains so when the fog sets it, it doesn't leave until next spring.

It would take me a decade before I realized my unworthiness and anxiety was connected to the split. You might be reading this and thinking, *Of course, silly you. Every psychology book says that.*

It's different when it's you though. It's easier to buy into the misunderstanding that you're this special snowflake and experiencing pain in a way no one's ever experienced it before. Even though this gives you great ammunition in the game of suffering and victim consciousness, it is the same thing that blocks your healing. Unlike Fyodor Dostoyevsky, a nineteenth-century Russian novelist, I think we are similar in our suffering, where we differ is in our joy.

We differ in the unique creations we bring to the world. In the way our unique soul blueprint shines through our life. In the way we choose to show up as an individuated soul. In the way we choose to move through this plane and on this planet called Earth. In the way we sing our song.

I think he was wrong. There are only so many ways to be sad but countless ways to be happy.

Now back to my unique sadness.

I went from a happy, bubble, social butterfly, A-student, to an almost-failing-out-of-school, depressed, crying-myself-to-sleep, wanting to die, anxiety ball, shell of myself. I was so afraid of being wrong and making a mistake that I **stopped speaking.**

I would stand on the sidelines and just listen—too afraid to say something wrong and have others see me. That is the exact opposite of my soul blueprint. I'm designed to shine, to stand at the forefront, to connect with people. So even though I felt "safe," I felt like my soul was ripped into a million pieces.

As the leaves fell, I longed for a way out. It couldn't stay this way forever.

WINTER

In Slovenian winter you forget what happiness feels like. Everything is dark and dreary. There's half melted snow, black from all the soot. No leaves, no birds, no sunshine. Although it feels like the end, it is also the darkness before dawn.

The birth canal. When we think nothing is going on, there's great activity right below the surface. This is where my healing began.

My first glimpse into, *It might not actually all be my fault* was discovering a video that highlighted three ways students react to a low grade.

Group one blames the teacher or the circumstances. "She's unfair. The test is unfair. I had the wrong pen." Group two blames themselves and who they are, at the core. "I'm just too stupid to succeed." Group three blames their actions and actions can be adjusted. "I could have prepared better and I will do so next time."

At the core, I had bought into the fixed mindset paradigm. This is a concept introduced by Stanford professor and researcher Carol Dweck: our qualities, like intelligence and resourcefulness, are fixed and unchanging. The opposite of that is the growth mindset, where you believe that your abilities can be developed and cultivated.

This fixed mindset was in part created by compliments and punishments for "who I am" and not "what I do." "Good job, you're so smart!" or "Wow, stop that! You're so horrible, no one will ever play with you!" instead of "Good job, I celebrate the way you showed up to this!" and "I don't like what you're doing."

This internalized parenting created a paradigm of belief that who I am is unchanging, which creates fear of being in a condition where my good qualities can be challenged. For example, I'm not smart anymore if I fail a test, so I'd rather just not try.

While embracing the fact that I might not be broken, I also found a great spiritual teacher named Alexander Palienko who helped me see how dark my thoughts were, and when I changed them, my whole countenance changed. Piece by piece I reclaimed myself. I did thought work and trigger work and trauma release. I wrote down all of my dysfunctional thoughts and replaced them with ones my higher self would believe.

It was all new and unfamiliar, but it felt like a soothing balm on my cracked soul. That brings me the most pride, showing up when I felt completely broken. Doing things when I believed subconsciously I was worthless. The courage and dedication it took to go against the grain, when few people were showing me what was possible, and most chose to dissociate.

There were other people who made me believe there was light at the end of the tunnel, like my athletic trainer, Lucas.

But healing isn't linear.

Even though I made great progress from the shell of a person I had been, I was still insecure and playing it small. I was part of a tennis team with a mentally and emotionally abusive coach. Even though what he did was totally wrong, in hindsight I can see how he was there to show me where I was allowing myself to be mistreated. Where I still believed I "deserved it" because I wasn't doing "good enough."

By reporting him to the school authorities and detailing exactly how he overstepped and abused his power, I reclaimed a part of myself.

This is where I expected my life to magically get better and get back to the way it was before it fell apart. I had been working hard, facing my fears, working on my shadow, why was I not there yet?

Instead, just as my head got above water, the Covid-19 pandemic hit. It created huge upheaval in my psyche - being isolated, not agreeing with how the situation was handled, the growing tensions in society.

I kept growing slowly, yet afraid to step into my full power.

SUMMER

Summers in Ljubljana can get hot, over a hundred degrees Fahrenheit. It's the perfect pressure cooker.

The last stretch, the last mile.

What did I do to deserve this? I thought to myself. *I've been doing the work to get better, when will I get there?*

Just a few days prior, I had taken a substance meant to help me relax after an interaction with my mom. Instead, it sent me on a ten-hour journey into the deepest, darkest crevices of my mind. Reliving my deepest, darkest fears, over and over. Stuck in regret, forever.

At the point where I decided I could not resist the darkness anymore, let go, and decided I am okay to die, it started dissipating. A true experience of surrender.

But in the days that followed, it felt like someone had turned my nervous system inside out. I was experiencing post traumatic stress disorder (PTSD).

Life is hell and I'm living it.

A part of me knew this was happening *for* me, for my greater good. Even though I had done a lot of work, there was still a chasm between my being and my fullest life experience.

No matter how terrible I felt, there was a lesson for me to learn, and the lesson was facing my fears can't possibly be worse than what I'm feeling right now.

So I started. *Slowly.*

One post on Instagram where I shared about my depression.

One post where I expressed my "controversial" views on men/women dynamics.

One post about my views on the pandemic.

One post of me dancing, mimicking an exotic dancer.

One post of me speaking on Orgasmic Birth and a reclamation through Instagram. How fitting.

I did all the things I was so afraid of doing, letting people who I knew and didn't really know, how I **really** felt.

Except nothing happened. I got a disagreeing comment here and there but nothing severe. Once my first experiment was successful, I ran some more. I signed up to be an Ecstatic Dance facilitator. You can ask any of my high school friends if a dance party was my worst nightmare.

Where do I put my hands? I feel so awkward. *What am I doing?*

There was a time where just dancing by myself at home in the bathroom made me uncomfortable, let alone when people were watching.

Signed up, did it, one of the most healing experiences of my life. Fear faced and I survived. Gee, this is actually fun.

Started a YouTube channel. Announced my business, oh boy. Struggled, found support. Faced my edges by investing in myself and being vulnerable about my insecurities in large groups.

Faced my dysfunctional patterns of perfectionism and believing that nothing is better than something. Bought into *Tiny Habits.* Stopped waiting for a perfect moment and started creating. Let go of the idea that I "failed" and accepted myself exactly as I am.

SPRING

The sun started shining again. Finally, after ten years of darkness that felt like it would never stop, I felt the sunshine on my face.

I now take my pace. I can't remember the last time I engaged in self-harm or self-loathing thoughts. I communicate with my family and enjoy a deep and loving committed relationship. I create daily and run my own business. I work with dream clients and help bring the light I wanted someone else to bring me.

I am happy.

As humans, our biggest need is to be accepted for **exactly who we are,** with our flaws and all. **To be witnessed** in all our weirdness,, in our darkest, loneliest, most despicable hour and *still be loved.*

The hardest part of this journey was that I looked like the person who "should have it all together." That I wasn't allowed to "complain." But just because you "have it all" doesn't mean you're not allowed to struggle.

Trauma doesn't care how pretty you are, or how much money you have, or if you like living in a first-world country or not. The funny thing is, it might not even be **your** trauma, but latent generational dysfunctional patterns that got triggered by an uncomfortable situation.

In my situation, it was divorce and moving. It could have been anything else. Sexual abuse. War. A bad break up. The point is not to avoid pain. It's learning how to be with it.

That's why it is essential to bring the healing art, spiritual arts, and understanding of the human psyche into the forefront. We are not robots.

We all suffer trauma. When it doesn't get addressed and processed, it snowballs. We are in a collective process of realizing the snowball isn't as unmanageable or random or dangerous as it seems.

It's just millions of little, hurt, unheard children crying out for love and attention. Let's give ourselves that love. Starting with one person at a time. You can't change the world, but you can change yourself. Through that, you change the future.

This Book Gives Back

For *Heal to Lead: Stories To Turn Your Wounds Into Wisdom* Volume One, we give one-hundred percent of all net proceeds to the Nashville Sexual Assault Center (SAC), where our publisher Raven and Grace Press is headquartered.

Nashville Sexual Assault Center provides healing for children, adults, and families affected by sexual assault and aims to end sexual violence through counseling, education, and advocacy.

In 1978, SAC was started by two Vanderbilt University divinity students who saw a need to help victims of rape and sexual abuse. Their vision was to provide support to all survivors of sexual assault and work to end sexual violence. SAC has operated in several locations over the years with a fire destroying the building and files in 1988. A permanent site was established in 1997 at 25 Lindsley Avenue in Nashville, Tennessee. In 2008, SAC moved to a new location at 101 French Landing where they continue to operate.

Due to recent growth, SAC now has more robust services including a clinical department, an Advocacy, SAFE Clinic and Hotline Team, a statewide training team, and a prevention and outreach team. SAC also provides medical-legal rape exams onsite in partnership with Sexual Assault Nurse Examiners from Nashville General Hospital. The SAFE Clinic was created after several years of multidisciplinary teamwork around improving the city's coordinated response to rape victims.

SAC is committed to providing the most effective services that empower individuals to overcome the effects of sexual assault. The clinical staff focuses on providing services to all victims of sexual assault including men, women, and children, regardless of their ability to pay. In addition, all staff remain committed to providing a safe, welcoming environment for all regardless of age, ethnicity, culture, gender, gender identity, sexual orientation, socioeconomic status or disability. For more information, visit SAC at https://sacenter.org/.

The authors of this book have created a digital workbook to accompany this book, filled with valuable tools to support your own journey. You'll find journal prompts to help you gain clarity, guided meditations to nurture your soul, and transformational educational videos designed to inspire your growth. To download the free workbook, visit https://ravenandgrace.com/healtolead1.